RHYMES
OF THE
RANGES

RHYMES OF THE RANGES

A New Collection of the Poems of

BRUCE KISKADDON

Edited and with an Introduction by

HAL CANNON

Illustrations by Katherine Field

GIBBS M. SMITH, INC.
PEREGRINE SMITH BOOKS
SALT LAKE CITY

This is a Peregrine Smith Book

Copyright © 1987 by Gibbs M. Smith, Inc.

Published 1987 by Gibbs M. Smith, Inc.
P.O. Box 667, Layton, Utah 84041

Jacket designed by J. Scott Knudsen
Printed and bound in the United States of America

91 90 89 88 87 5 4 3 2 1

FIRST EDITION

Library of Congress Cataloging-in-Publication Data

Kiskaddon, Bruce, 1878–1949.
    Rhymes of the ranges.

    1. Cowboys—Poetry. 2. Ranch life—Poetry.
3. West (U.S.—Poetry. I. Cannon, Hal, 1948–
II. Title.
PS3521.I764R5 1987   811'.52   86–31334
ISBN 0-87905-264-3

Contents

Bruce Kiskaddon: Cowboy Poet

There's no darker place than at the edge of the spotlight.

Bruce Kiskaddon is America's premier cowboy poet, though he spent the last third of his life as a bellhop in Los Angeles hotels. He may have carried bags for Roy Rogers, John Wayne, Gene Autry, or Ronald Reagan; but his words will live more profoundly than any of theirs as a document of the American cowboy.

Kiskaddon never participated in the "Southern California cowboy" scene of movie stars, parade saddles, cowboy songs in four-part harmony, or restored ranchos along the coast. He understood that the popular cowboy image obscured the life he loved—the real world of beef cows, horses, and cowmen. His life was modest. His homes were a series of pastel Spanish adobe houses in blue collar neighborhoods, on streets lined with tall palms. Every day he put on his pressed "monkey uniform" and went to work at the Mayflower Hotel in downtown Los Angeles. Between calls, he sat in the corner of the lobby with a stubby pencil in hand and opened up a world of memory—of cow camps, horses, and open land. As he wrote, the words came in rhyme:

> I can see the East is gettin' gray.
> I'll gather the hosses soon;
> And faint from the valley far away
> Comes the drone of the last guard's tune.
> Yes, life is just like the night-herd's song,
> As the long years come and go.
> You start with a swing that is free and strong,
> And finish up tired and slow.
>
> **"The Old Night Hawk"**

Bruce Kiskaddon (1878–1950) was born in Pennsylvania, later moving to southern Colorado near Trinidad. He started riding the Picket Wire district in 1898. Into the l920s, he worked off and on for cow and horse outfits in the American Southwest and in Australia. In the summer of 1922, he worked for a time for G.T. (Tap) Duncan in northwestern Arizona. Duncan, noticing Kiskaddon's talent for parody and for making up little jingles during the course of the day's work, insisted that Kiskaddon try writing some Western verse. By 1924, Kiskaddon had published a small book of poems entitled *Rhymes of the Ranges*.

After returning to Arizona from Australia in the mid-twenties, he and some of his cowboy friends heard there were good-paying jobs in Hollywood riding horses in the movies. On impulse, they went to Hollywood in 1926 and got jobs driving chariots in the original silent version of *Ben Hur*.

This was the Prohibition Era, and access to spirits was not easy. One night as the cowboys sat around their hotel room, they asked a bellhop to get them some whiskey. When he returned, he handed the bottle over and stated the price. Kiskaddon sat up with a start and asked how much of the exorbitant price was the tip. The man answered casually that he figured a dollar from each of the cowboys. Kiskaddon said, ''That sounds like a job for me,'' and the next morning got a job as a bellboy.

For the rest of his life, Bruce Kiskaddon lived in Los Angeles, where he married and had a daughter. He had loved his life as a cowhand, but knew it was a young man's job, and one that was hard on families. In spirit, though, he continued to ride the range; and as the years went by, he could never get his life as a cowboy out of his mind.

Although you return to the city
And mingle again with the throng;
Though your heart may be softened by pity,
Or bitter from strife and wrong.

Though others should laugh in derision,
And the voice of the past grow dim,
Yet, stick to the cool decision
That you made on the mountain's rim.

"The Time to Decide"

We have no more than a brief outline of the remainder of
Bruce Kiskaddon's life. He continued to write poetry, and
carried his work down to the Union Stockyards each month
where he sold the poems to Nelson Crow, publisher of
Western Livestock. The poems were sent to Katherine Field
at her family's ranch in central New Mexico to be illustrated,
before being published in the monthly magazine.

The combination of Kiskaddon's poems and Katherine
Field's illustrations was magic. Although the poems did not
reach the huge audiences who listened to cowboy songs, and
the illustrations did not hang in the salons of the
banker/ranchers who bought the artwork of Remington and
Russell, these works and visual images went to the heart of
cattle country. On the rural-route ranches, families would
eagerly thumb through *Western Livestock* each month to
find the new illustrated Kiskaddon poem. The popularity of
these poems is suggested by their frequent appearance in the
scrapbooks of multi-generation cattle operations. Among the
photos of prize bulls, winning local bronc riders, and kids
riding off to the first day of school, are carefully clipped
poems by Bruce Kiskaddon illustrated by Katherine Field.

Katherine Field was born about 1899 near Magdalena, New
Mexico. As a young girl, she contracted polio which left her
crippled. Living on a large New Mexico ranch as a crippled

child must have been hard, though I've heard it said that ranch kids learn to walk late because riding always comes first. This was absolutely true for Katherine, and she was always at home on horseback. Her family remembers that she always had a great love and admiration for horses. She loved to draw them. As she grew older, her artistic talents grew, and she started drawing scenes from the life around her. Frank King, who wrote a popular gossip column for *Western Livestock*, was impressed with her talents and encouraged her to send her work to the magazine.

Katherine had married a young Navajo, John Guerro, who worked at the ranch. They needed money, so she began illustrating Kiskaddon's poems. For each illustration she was paid ten dollars, and Kiskaddon was probably paid about the same amount. Though they never met, they both understood the western land and ranch life. A mutual respect developed between them which lasted until their deaths, less than a year apart.

* * *

Kiskaddon's poetry was intended to be read aloud, for it is essentially an oral literature first. Written, it lacks uniform poetic convention; but recited, it shows a highly developed complexity which provides a subtle interplay between rhythm, rhyme, and meaning. Literary critics commonly dismiss it as doggerel, but from a listener's point of view, it has appealing attributes. It is beautifully crafted within a literary tradition which puts a high premium on precise form and vivid language. It is folk poetry, too, because its form and rhythm are part of an old tradition well understood by its practitioners.

I have asked cowboys and ranchers what it is about Bruce Kiskaddon's poetry that is so fine. What makes his poems so valued? Typically they tell me, "Kiskaddon tells it like it is." In other words, he shares the rare and treasured knowledge of his occupational group. He is so successful, that cowboys over the past fifty years have learned and relearned his poems. They have been recited in bars and on cow ranches from California to Kansas. Often the poems are passed around without the cowboys' knowing the author's name. And even those who know it don't pronounce it in a standard way. Sometimes it is Kiss-K-Dun, or Kis-Ca-Doon, or Kis-Ca-Dun.

In the introduction to a book he published shortly before his death, Kiskaddon stated: "My powers of imagination are not what some writers are gifted with. So you will find these rhymes are all written from actual happenings or from the old legends of the cow country." His modest reliance on the facts of range life is what sets him apart from the Western writers of the day whose romanticized tales generally misrepresent the cowboy.

Probably the most often recited of Kiskaddon's poems is "The Little Blue Roan." It tells of a cowboy about to brand an unmarked heifer. The cowboy tells how his little horse keeps watching some piñon trees in the distance as he prepares to put his brand on another man's animal. The horse's uneasiness makes him decide to brand the heifer with the same brand that is on her mother standing nearby. As he does, two cowmen emerge from the piñon trees, but, seeing that everything is right with the branding, they all sit for a sociable smoke. A potentially explosive situation has been averted by the warning from the horse.

This poem bursts with potential drama and emotion. Yet, it is so intensely understated that, to the casual reader, it might seem barely to hold together. It has great meaning only to someone who shares intimately the significance of a brand, the complicated ethics of cattlemen, cowboy language, and the love of a horse. Characteristically, Kiskaddon believes it takes such personal experience to read between the lines:

> *The joys as clear as the morning—*
> *The tortures akin to hell.*
> *They never will reach outsiders*
> *Who were raised in the town's confines;*
> *But they're here for the hard old riders,*
> *Who can read them between the lines.*

"Between the Lines"

This kind of shared knowledge is at the heart of folk art, for effective folk art depends most deeply on communicating the shared experiences of the group that produces it.

Another important aspect of folk art is its usefulness as a teacher of informal skills. I have never encountered an occupation which requires so much skill for so little pay as that of a cowboy. There is no classwork or manual to teach these skills. They must be learned by apprenticeship or imitation, by hearing or reading stories, or by other forms of close personal interaction. Many of Kiskaddon's shorter poems, which originally appeared as a monthly feature of *Western Livestock* and were printed on the backs of Union Stockyard Auction circulars, hold hidden lessons on the art of being a good cowboy, of "making a hand."

> *Nice new clo'es purtects the hide*
> *And sorter contents a man inside.*
> *Clo'es does a heap toward makin' the man.*
> *Try goin' without and you'll onderstand.*

"All Dressed Up"

Kiskaddon wrote three basic kinds of poems. His early poems generally tell a story. They are relatively long and have been popular as memorized recitations. The original *Rhymes of the Ranges*, published in 1924, and his last book, the enlarged *Rhymes of the Ranges and Other Poems* (1947), contain many of these narrative works. *Western Poems*, published by *Western Livestock* in 1935, contains shorter poems first published by the magazine. These verses, almost all illustrated by Katherine Field, fit into two basic categories. Some deal with the environment in an impressionistic way, while others are situational, often including very dry cowboy humor. A fourth book of shorter poems, called *Just As Is*, had little distribution.

Until recently, Bruce Kiskaddon has been known and loved only by the people of the West who appreciate and live ranch life. He has never been recognized by scholars of Western literature or folklore. He was a commercial poet who had to support his family by the tips of travelers. Feeling out of place in the modern world, he found refuge in memories and experience. He was private in his personal life, but as a poet he elicited for many an entire cultural heritage.

> *I'll ride the trail till the stars turn pale*
> *And camp at the break of dawn,*
> *Nobody will know which way I go,*
> *They'll only know I'm gone.*
>
> **"I'm Hittin' the Trail Tonite"**

Wheaton Hale Brewer, in his foreword to *Western Poems*, was prophetic when he wrote: "The true poet is he whose poetry rings true—as Bruce's poems ring true. He has lived the life of which he writes—a life which rapidly is vanishing, its people already taking to themselves the qualities of legend and high romance. . . . As the years roll on and history appreciates the folk-lore of the plains and ranges, these poems by a real cowboy will take on deeper significance and mightier stature." The years have rolled on, and Bruce Kiskaddon and his words take on renewed meaning for a new generation of people who love the open lands of the West.

> Yes, that was the bundle stiff, shunned and
>   neglected.
> A child of the old West; her youngest and last.
> She handed him nothing, just as he expected,
> When he took the dim trail that led into the past.

"The Bundle Stiff"

HAL CANNON

Acknowledgments

Bruce Kiskaddon was a private man. His poems were the documents of his life. Nelson Crow, publisher of *Western Livestock*, and countless cowboys who learned the poems and passed them around the West are to be thanked for bringing Kiskaddon's work to us. The power of his poetry continues to reverberate through the ranching West.

I first heard the poems recited by Waddie Mitchell. I began to realize the impact this poetry has had on cowboys and ranchers through the work of folklorist Gary Stanton. The few things we know about Kiskaddon's life came from Dick Crow, current publisher of *Western Livestock*.

Thanks to Kurt Markus, Cyd McMullen, and Joni Santini for their help with this effort. Particular thanks go to John Guerro who shared information about his first wife, Katherine Field, with me during a visit to the Alamo Navajo Reservation in 1984.

The poems selected for this book have come from the out-of-print books of Bruce Kiskaddon and from scrapbooks of ranchers who collected his poems—in particular from the collections of Walter Meyer, Arthur Glaser, and Ellen Faye McFarlane.

The cover art came from a sketchbook of the Wyoming painter, Minerva Teichert, and was graciously lent to us by Mr. and Mrs. Hamilton Teichert. Illustrations in the book are by Katherine Field. The jacket was designed by J. Scott Knudsen.

After the Fall Roundup

Now the summer work is over and the wagon's pullin' in,
And we've said good bye to fellers that we mightn't see agin,
Fer a cow boy don't write letters so we mighty soon lose track
Of the boys that stops and works a while and never does come
    back.

When yore clothes is soter tattered and yore hat brim sags and
    flops,
And yore boots is wore and battered, them that had the fancy
    tops,
When the owners and the bosses and the hands is most all in.
And then strings of summer hosses is slowed up and lookin'
    thin.

When them thin clouds start a trailin through the soft and
   pleasant sky,
And you watch old buzzard sailin' soter useless way up high,
And it makes the toughest cow boy soter study after all,
When he's draggin' with the wagon to the home ranch in the
   fall.

Fer he caint help but remember that most cow boys don't git
   old
And he'll git to one November when he caint stand work and
   cold;
He shore knows that he'll be sorry when he gits like you and me;
Jest an old man tellin' stories 'bout how good he used to be.

Alkali Ike's Zippers

"Now speakin' of Zippers," sez Alkali Ike,
"Them zippers is sumpthin' I really don't like.
I aimed to buy clothes like I always had wore,
Till I started a lookin' around in the store.

They had some new shirts and some new overalls.
That fastened with zippers, no buttons aytall.
I reckoned that clothes with a riggin' like that
Would be fine fer the boys on the Alkali Flat.

Because where there's alkali water to drink,
Things may happen sooner than what you might think.
So I got me some clothes that was rigged up like that,
And went back to my camp on the Alkali Flat.
Next mornin' I'd traveled fer mebby a mile,
When the time come to give them new zippers a trial.
I grabbed at the handle and give 'em a jerk
But holey old golden them zippers don't work.

I swear and I sweat, I am shore out of luck.
I have started 'em crooked, the zipper is stuck.
I fuss and I pull till I git the thing straight,
Then the zipper it works, but a little too late.

The next thing I do is to throw them new garments
Up onto a cactus fer ants and fer varmints.
And I reckon that buttons is safer at that,
Fer fellers that lives on the Alkali Flat.

All Dressed Up

Things is pickin' up as most folks knows,
So I sent to town fer to git new clo'es.
Some onderwear and a big hat box,
A couple of shirts and a passel of socks.

Some overalls and other truck,
Three red bandannys throwed in fer luck.
My boots aint new but they'll do right well,
I reckon I'll make them last a spell.

I'll be the pride of the whole derned spread
With a fust class Stetson on my head.
A bran new slicker tied on behind—
It's strange how yore clo'es improves yore mind.

Nice new clo'es purtects the hide
And sorter contents a man inside.
Clo'es does a heap toward makin' the man.
Try goin' without and you'll onderstand.

Alone

The hills git awful quiet, when you have to camp alone.
It's mighty apt to set a feller thinkin'.
You always half way waken when a hoss shoe hits a stone,
Or you hear the sound of hobble chains a clinkin'.

It is then you know the idees that you really have in mind.
You think about the things you've done and said.
And you sometimes change the records that you nearly always
      find
In the back of almost every cow boy's head.

It gives a man a soter different feelin' in his heart.
And he sometimes gits a little touch of shame,
When he minds the times and places that he didn't act so smart,
And he knows himself he played a sorry game.

It kinda makes you see yourself through other people's eyes.
And mebby so yore pride gits quite a fall.
When yore all alone and thinkin', well, you come to realize
Yo're a mighty common feller after all.

The Bargain

When a cow boy and Indian meet on the range,
Perhaps they're acquainted, perhaps they are strange.
They both will slow down till they ride at a walk;
When they git close together they stop fer a talk.

The Indian waits, fer the Indian knows,
That a white man wants somethin' wherever he goes.
White men are like that any where on the earth
And they start in by offerin' half what it's worth.

So the Indian knows he is sartin to find
About what the cow puncher has on his mind.
Perhaps it's a hoss trade he's trying to make,
Perhaps it's a message he wants him to take.

He lets the cow puncher put on the whole show.
He doesn't say yes and he doesn't say no.
All through the whole bargain the Injun sits tight,
Till he makes him an offer he thinks is all right.

Between the Lines

There's something I'm not forgetting,
But it's something I could not say.
I could not arrange the setting
And the scene, in the proper way.
The air of the desert and mountain,
The smoke of the far out camp,
The whispering voice of the night wind
And the picketed horse's tramp.
The tread of the moving cattle,
The song that the riders croon,
The swing and the sway of the saddle
That goes to the lilt of the tune.
The race after wild young horses
That beats any hunt for game;
The battle of wits and forces
Until the wild brutes are tame.
For the strong young steeds are fighters
That are raised on the hills and plains,

They must learn to balance their riders;
You must teach them to answer the reins.
It calls for skillful riders,
Your hardiest strongest men;
The buck and bawl, the sickening fall,
And the whirl of the broncho pen.
The rush of the summer branding
When the work is rough and hard,
Beyond all understanding,
And the shivering nights on guard.
The quiet night in the summer
When the air is moist and warm;
You hear the rumbling thunder
And watch the approaching storm.
When the heavens pour like a funnel
And the Devil his own can claim;
When the sky is black as a tunnel,
Then white with the lightening's flame.
It is then that the weak go under;
It calls for a hardy breed.
The shattering crash of the thunder
And the rush of the mad stampede.
The terrible grip of the blizzard
When the horse and rider reel.
The curse of the snow blind puncher,
And the frost bites that throb and peel.
The nights you hate to remember
When you lay in the line camp alone
When the gray wolves howled in the timber
And the perishing cattle moaned.
You tried to prevent the slaughter,
But the frost and the storm were king.
How you chopped the ice from the water
And prayed for an early spring.
Or down in the desert regions
And the ranges far to the south.

Where the cattle swarm in legions
And the stock man is caught in the drouth.
Springs are steadily failing
Almost no place to go.
Coyotes are always wailing,
Buzzards are circling low.
What once were strong young cattle
Are only suffering wrecks,
So thin that they seem to rattle
When you stick your knife in their necks.
Cattle too weak to gather-
You must try it although you fail;
Holding them up in the "Prather"
"Chousing" them over the trail.
On every side they are crying,
"Take your cattle away;
Half of our own are dying-
No water and grass for strays."

Cow-boys in clothing tattered,
Faces and hands brush scarred,
Saddles and chaps all battered,
Horses look gaunt and hard.
The heat and the dust that smothers,
The tired out horse that lags,
The calves that have lost their mothers
Wailing along in the drags.

That's why I'm giving you warning—
There's something I cannot tell.
The joys as clear as the morning
The tortures akin to Hell.
They never will reach outsiders
Who were raised in the town's confines,
But they're here for the hard old riders
Who can read them between the lines.

A Boy's Friend

You can mind an old feller that shore made you mad.
He would ask you fool questions and wink at yore dad.
It allus did give him a special delight
To make fun of sumpthin' you hadn't done right.

But the day you got lost and was ready to bawl,
He found you, and wasn't so bad after all.
He laffed at you shore, but you mind to this day,
The things that he told 'bout findin' yore way.

Once you upset a wagon. He helped you reload.
He fetched back your saddle one time you got throwed.
When you took yore first job and was ready to quit,
He ribbed you until you took holt of the bit.

One day you got into a fight and got licked;
And the feller bulldozed you until you was sick.
But the old man laffed at you and made you so mad
That you went back and licked him and beat him up bad.

When yore gal turned you down, he rawhided yore back,
Till you cornered that gal and got down to brass tacks.
You found out she liked you right down in her heart,
Then the old feller staked you and give you yore start.

It had been quite a number of years since you cried,
But you bawled like a baby the day that he died.
Yes, yore Father and Mother was kind, that is true;
But that ribbin' old cuss made a man out of you.

Katherine Field - 35

The Brandin' Corral

When the west was all onsettled and there wasn't no bob
  wire,
They had a way of workin' that was supthin' to admire.
Every thing was done on hoss back, and I've heard old
  timers talk
How the kids in cattle countries didn't hardly learn to walk.

They worked cattle in the open, and they laid 'em on the
  ground.
It was cuttin', flankin', ropin', and a tyin' critters down.
But the present cattle raiser aint so strong fer that idee,
And he has a way of workin' that's as different as can be.

'Taint so hard on men and hosses, and it's better fer cow
  brutes
When you got a place to work 'em in corrals and brandin'
  chutes.
When we heard of brandin' fluid, fust we took it fer a
  joke.
Jest to think of brandin' cattle when you couldn't smell no
  smoke.

21

Well a feller caint deny it that the new way is the best.
Fer there's been a heap of changes in the ranges of the
     west.
Most of outfits then was bigger, and a cow was jest a cow,
And they didn't stop to figger things as close as they do
     now.

The Broncho Twister's Prayer

It was a little grave yard on the rolling foot hill plains:
That was bleached by the sun in summer, swept by winter's
    snows and rains;
There a little bunch of settlers gathered on an autumn day
'Round a home made lumber coffin, with their last respects to
    pay.

Weary men that wrung their living from that hard and arid
    land,
And beside them stood their women; faded wives with toil
    worn hands.
But among us stood one figure that was wiry, straight and trim.
Every one among us knew him. 'Twas the broncho twister, Jim.

Just a bunch of hardened muscle tempered with a savage grit,
And he had the reputation of a man that never quit.
He had helped to build the coffin, he had helped to dig the
    grave;
And his instinct seemed to teach him how he really should
    behave.

Well, we didn't have a preacher, and the crowd was mighty
    slim.
Just two women with weak voices sang an old time funeral
    hymn.
That was all we had for service. The old wife was sobbing
    there.
For her husband of a life time, laid away without prayer.

She looked at that broncho twister, then she walked right up to him.
Put one trembling arm around him and said "Pray. Please won't you Jim?"
You could see his figure straighten, and a look of quick surprise
Flashed across his swarthy features, and his hard dare devil eyes.

He could handle any broncho, and he never dodged a fight.
'Twas the first time any body ever saw his face turn white.
But he took his big sombrero off his rough and shaggy head,
How I wish I could remember what that broncho peeler said.

No, he wasn't educated. On the range his youth was spent.
But the maker of creation knew exactly what he meant.
He looked over toward the mountains where the driftin' shadows played.
Silence must have reigned in heaven when they heard the way Jim prayed.

Years have passed since that small funeral in that lonely grave yard lot.
But it gave us all a memory, and a lot of food for thought.
As we stood beside the coffin, and the freshly broken sod,
With that reckless broncho breaker talkin' heart to heart with God.

When the prayer at last was over, and the grave had all been filled,
On his rough, half broken pony, he rode off toward the hills.
Yes, we stood there in amazement as we watched him ride away,
For no words could ever thank him. There was nothing we could say.

Since we gathered in that grave yard, it's been nearly fifty years.
With their joys and with their sorrows, with their hopes and with their fears.
But I hope when I have finished, and they lay me with the dead,
Some one says a prayer above me, like that broncho twister said.

The Bundle Stiff

Can you feature a man with no home and no neighbors,
And often no roof that would cover his head?
Who lived by the roughest and hardest of labor
And carried the blankets that served for his bed.

He lived on the cheapest and coarsest of rations.
They worked him long hours for miserable pay.
Though his was the work helped develop the nation,
He was always unwelcome and sent on his way.

He helped to build railroads, he helped to dig ditches,
He helped to build bridges, he graded the road.
But all of it brought him no leisure or riches;
On the highways he built he could walk with his load.

Too sullen for fear and too hardened for pity
He worked with the toilers and travelled with tramps.
His soul had been seared by the sins of the city,
His body was hard from his toil in the camps.

In the cities the parisites hounded him, craving
To get their vile hands on what money he made.
To steal the few dollars he'd gathered by slaving
In the gloom of the mine or the dust of the grade.

The buffalo hunter, the trapper, the trader.
They roamed through the West and collected their spoil.
But all that the bundle stiff got was hard labor
While other men reaped the result of his toil.

The cow boy was famous in song and in story.
Of the trooper and scout you hear many a tale.
But into his life came no honor or glory;
'Twas hunger that drove on the bundle stiff's trail.

Speak not of the Hindu oh misguided dreamer.
Nor scorn his belief with its casts and its cults.
You live in a nation that worshipped the schemer
And sneered at the man who obtained the results.

I ask for no statue in heroic mould
Of Labor performing some gigantic task,
Of the trades of the empires, the arts have oft told
But this for the stiff with his bundle I ask.

Show a broad shouldered man that is weary and jaded
And slung from his shoulder a roughly made pack
In ill fitting clothes that are battered and faded
As he trudges along on the road or the track.

Yes, that was the bundle stiff, shunned and neglected.
A child of the old West; her youngest and last.
She handed him nothing, just as he expected,
When he took the dim trail that led into the past.

The Bunk House Mirror

That old bunk house mirror that most of us knew.
I remember it yet, and I know that you do.
One corner broke out, and sort of a crack
That run half way across and a quarter way back.
The cheap wooden frame with the varnish all gone,
But the grease and the dirt and the fly specks stayed on.

And then the quicksilver was missin' in spots,
But that didn't bother a cow hand a lot.
He picked the good places and managed to shave
As he looked at his face in the ripples and waves,
No wonder the mirror was terribly wrecked
When you thought of the faces it had to reflect.

And the comb that hung down from a string underneath.
It was chuck full of gum though it lacked a few teeth.
And there on the bench was a rusty wash pan
Where we smeared yeller soap on our faces and hands.
The bosses them days didn't go fer expense.
You could buy the whole outfit fer ninety five cents.

But boy let me tell you that old lookin' glass
Has reflected the faces of men with a past.
I wonder it didn't back up with surprise
If it read what was lurkin' just back of their eyes.
I will bet there's a lot of old hands can recall
The battered old mirror that hung on the wall.

Katherine Field _35.

A Calf's Troubles

A calf don't do no workin, all he does is stick around.
And his mother has to feed him till some other feed is
      found.
He starts in havin' trouble shortly after he is born;
They rope him and they brand him, and he likely gits
      dehorned.

And then they take the markin' knife and whittle on his
      ears,
Till them "Crops" and "Forks" will mark him if he lives
      fer twenty years.
While the brand is still a hurtin' and the dust is in his eye,
They take and vaccinate him so he dassent even die.

And when he's big enough fer beef they knock him in the
      head.
That's the end of all his troubles, fer after that he's dead.
There's now and then a feller that is jest a lot like that.
You never find him workin' no matter where he's at.

He seems to git off easy. All he does is eat and sleep,
But nobody don't respect him and he has to take a heap.
And you'll mostly find a feller that aint a bit of use,
Is so lazy and so callous that he'd rather take abuse.

Katharine Field - 1935.

Caught Nappin'

You caint exactly figger what a half broke hoss will do.
When a feller aint a thinkin' that's jest when he breaks in
    two.
You are throwed before you know it, and when he gits you
    down,
He keeps buckin' with your saddle till you're glad you're on
    the ground.

He aint hurt you none to speak of, but you're well shook
    up at that,
And you caint git up to ketch him till he's foggin down the
    flat.
You know the place he waters, and it's safe enough to say,
He'll be with a bunch of hosses six or seven miles away.

You must take it "Poco poco" when you start your
    homeward walk.
Folks would think you'd gone plum loco if they listened to
    your talk.
You have got a grudge at bronchos so you cuss the buckin'
    brutes.
And your feet gits sore and blistered till you cuss your high-
    heeled boots.

29

You are tired, hot and thirsty. You git to the ranch half
    dead,
And of course them other fellers has to give up lots of
    head.
Everybody in the outfit seems to have a lot to say,
When a feller comes in walkin' and his hoss has got away.

The Christmas Tree

They've been to get their Christmas tree, they hadn't far to
    go.
They live in that high country where young timber starts to
    grow.
The day is cold the snow is new, there's not so many tracks.
The dad has got the Christmas tree, the kid he has the ax.

You notice by the chimney that the fire place is wide.
They have their house built strong and low, it's plenty
    warm inside.
They've got a set of good corrals besides a stable too;
They are fixed up pretty handy fer a place to winter
    through.

And when they put the candles on it's easy to believe
How that tree will look by fire light this comin' Christmas
    eve.
There won't be any carols sung, there won't no organ play
But they'll have a happy Christmas in them hills so far
    away.

I'll bet the old man's thinkin' back to when he was a kid.
How folks would spend their Christmas and the things he
    got and did.
Of course the kid, he looks ahead, he don't think of the
    past,
But he'll soon have Christmas memories that he'll keep
    until the last.

The Chuck Wagon

She ain't what she was in the days of her glory.
Fer years she has stood in the cotton wood shade.
But if she could talk, she could tell you some story,
Of her days on the range, and the part that she played.

The old mess box built in her back, is still standin'.
But the canvas is gone that we put on her bows.
Each year she went out fer the round up and brandin',
And came back from the beef hunt along with the snows.

When we got on the camp ground I sure did admire,
How the cook and the wrangler would onhitch the team.
Then they throwed the old dutch oven into the fire—
Them biscuits he baked I can taste in my dreams.

With the boys sleepin' 'round her she looked sort of lonely,
Like a small country church in a little grave yard.
But she looked plenty good when you slid off your pony,
When you came into camp fer to wake the next guard.

But the wagon was home and we gathered around her;
Chuck riders came in when the pickin's was short;
Some of 'em would eat till they'd mighty nigh founder—
It was there in the night we held kangaroo court.

I liked them old hands with their gaze cool and level.
They furnished the subject fer many a tale.
It was little they feared either man, beast or devil,
Them riders that follered the chuck wagon's trail.

But the time I liked best, as I clearly remember;
Is one every cow puncher likes to recall.
When the work was all finished along in November,
And he follered the chuck wagon home in the fall.

Cold Mornin's

I been out in the weather since I was a boy,
But cold mornin's is sumthin' a man caint enjoy.
It makes me feel like I wanted to quit
When I ketch up my pony and thaw out my bit.

There aint any cow puncher needs to be told
That my saddle is stiff and the leather is cold.
The blankets is froze and the hoss shakes like jelly
When you pull the old frozen cinch up on his belly.

He snorts and he's got a mean look in his eye.
He is humped till the back of the saddle stands high.
He aint in no humor to stand fer a joke.
But I belt on my chaps and I light me a smoke.

There may be some trouble between me and him.
It is like going into cold water to swim.
It gives me a sort of a shivver and scare
But once I git started; well then I don't care.

The Cow and the Calf

A cow and a calf, or a calf and a cow.
Either way that you say it, it don't matter how;
But there's the foundation of all the beef trade,
And it always has been since the first beef was made.

Calves may have had fathers or sisters and brothers,
But they wore the same brand that was put on their
      mothers.
If hundreds of cattle was mixed in a herd,
When a cow claimed a calf, the whole world took her word.

Folks thought more of calves than of children, they did.
In them days nobody adopted a kid,
But a whole lot of fellers jest couldn't be stopped,
If a calf was unbranded and there to adopt.

So you caint blame a cow fer the way she took care,
And fed and purtected her calf every where.
And the whole cattle business I'll tell you right now
Depended a heap on the sense of a cow.

Katherine Field – 38.

The Cowboys' Christmas Dance

Winter is here and it aint so nice tendin' the feeders and
    choppin' ice.
Nasty weather to stir about. Cold in the mornin's a gittin'
    out.
Puts a sting in your ears and nose; gotta watch out or you'll
    freeze yore toes.
Blowin' your breath on a frosty bit. Makes you feel like you
    want to quit.

You like one part of it any way, that's when you git yore
    Christmas day.
Plenty of feed and a right good chance to shake yore feet at
    a country dance.
Fiddles a playin' jest watch 'em go. "Aleman left an' doce
    do!"
Don't keer none fer the cold and storm. Dancin' around
    you soon git warm.

Folks all in from the hills and flats. Ears tied up in onder
  their hats.
Tough on the hosses they drove and rode shivverin' there
  with their backs all bowed.
It's the only time that folks has to spare so the hosses has
  got to stand their share.
You turn 'em out when they git rode down but you got to
  keep workin' the year around.

Winter time but it aint so bad. When it comes around yore
  sorter glad.
Even though it's nasty weather folks has a chance to git
  together.
And plenty of folks that was half way mad found out their
  neighbors was not so bad,
Yes lots of trouble is checked in advance by a sociable
  crowd at a Christmas dance.

The Cow Boy's Dream

A cow boy and his trusty pal
Were camped one night by an old corral;
They were keeping a line on the boss's steers
And looking for calves with lengthy ears.
The summer work was long since through
And only the winter branding to do.
When he went to rest there was frost on his bed
But he pulled the tarp over his head;
And into his blankets he burrowed deep,
He soon got warm and was fast asleep.
He dreamed he was through with his wayward past
And had landed safe in Heaven at last.

A city was there with its pearly gate
And the golden streets were wide and straight.
The marble palaces gleamed and shone
And the choir sang 'round the great white throne.
Outside there were trees and meadows green—
Such a beautiful range he had never seen,
Great rivers of purest waters flowed
Though it never rained nor it never snowed.

He stood aside on the golden street,
There were heavy spurs on his booted feet,
His bat wing chaps were laced with whang,
But he listened and looked while the angels sang.
He noticed he was the only one
With a broad brimmed hat and a big six gun.

So he said to a saint, "I'd shore admire
To be dressed like one of that angel choir,
Instead of these chaps and spurs and gun;
And I reckon as how it could be done."
So they took him into a room aside
And they fastened wings on his toughened hide.

They fitted him out with a flowing robe,
Like the lady who looks in the crystal globe.
They gave him a crown and a golden harp
And the frost lay thick on the cow boy's tarp.

He twanged his harp and he sang a while,
Then he thought of something that made him smile.
Said he "I reckon these wings would do
To show some mustangs a thing or two.
I'll jump a bunch and I'll yell and whoop,
I'll kick their tails and I'll flop and swoop;
I'll light a straddle of one of the things,
And I'll flop his flanks with my angel wings.
I'll ride him bare-back, but if I fail,
And he bucks me off, I'll simply sail."
He hunted wild horses in his dream,
But all he found was the charist team.
That Old Elija drove in there,
And to pick on them would hardly be fair.

So he seated himself beneath a tree
And rested his crown upon his knee.
He watched the beautiful angels go
Flying and fluttering to and fro.
At last one landed and started to walk,
She came up close and began to talk.
She had lovely hair of golden brown
And was dressed in a flimsy silken gown.
She had dimpled cheeks, her eyes were blue,
And her fair white skin was beautiful too.

The cow boy gazed at the angel's charms
And attempted to clasp her within his arms.
"Stop! Stop!" She cried, "Or I'll make complaints
To the great white throne and the ruling saints."
So the cow boy halted I must confess
And failed to bestow that fond caress.

Said he, "Miss Angel, It's shore too bad.
This sort of a country makes me sad.
Where there ain't no night and it's always day,
And the beautiful ladies won't even play.
Where there's wonderful houses and golden streets,
But nobody sleeps and nobody eats.
Them beautiful rivers, it's sad to think
There ain't no hosses or cows to drink.
With all this grass a goin' to seed
And there ain't no critters to eat the feed.

A man can't gamble—There's so much gold
He could pick up more than his clothes would hold.
What's the use of the Judge and the great white throne
Where troubles or fights was never known?
I'm sorry miss but I'll tell you true,
This ain't no place fer a buckaroo."

Then she asked him about his former life
And learned he had never possessed a wife.
But this angel lady so sweet and nice,
Informed him that she had been married twice.
Her husbands had both been quiet men
But if she had it to do again,
She'd have to decide between just two.
A sailor boy or a buckaroo.
She seated herself upon his knees
And gave his neck such a hearty squeeze—
Just then they heard an excited call,
'Twas a gray old saint on the city wall.

He flopped his robes and he waved his arm
Till the crowd all gathered in great alarm;
And then the cow boy stood alone,
Before the judge and the great white throne.

"What's this?" the Judge Of Creation cried.
"How come this fellow to get inside?
Age must be dimming St. Peter's eye
To let a spirit like that get by.
Just look at his face with its desert brown,
And his bandy legs 'neath his angel gown.
He's a buckaroo, I know them well,
They don't allow them even in Hell.
He hasn't been here a half a day
And he started an angel to go astray.
We can't permit him to stay atall.
Just pitch him over the outside wall."

So the saints and the angels gave him a start
And he went toward the Earth like a falling dart.
He never remembered the time he lit
For he wakened before the tumble quit.
The winter wind blew cold and sharp
And the frost lay thick on the cow boy's tarp.

His beautiful vision had come to grief,
So he baked his biscuits and fried some beef.
And drank some coffee black and strong;
But all that day as he rode along
He thought of the saint who had butted in,
And he said to himself with a wicked grin,
"I wish I had holt of that old saint chap,
I'd grab his whiskers and change his map.
I'd jump on his frame and I'd stomp aroun'
Till I tromped him out of his saintly gown."

And all his life as he roamed and toiled,
He thought of his vision so sadly spoiled.
And the meddlesome saint that had caused it all
When he gave the alarm from the Jasper wall.
He didn't repent nor he didn't pray,
But he always wished they had let him stay.

The Cow Boy's Shirt Tail

There is one thing people inquire about;
They ask why a cow puncher's shirt tail comes out.
Most any rough hand that you happen across—
If he's skinnin' a beef, if he's shoin' a hoss;
If he's ridin' a broncho or flankin' a calf—
Well, his shirt tail is out, or at least the last half.

Now workin' wild stock where the brush is right thick,
Where the cattle is sudden and cow boys is quick;
If you notice a man and a hoss disappear,
That is, if you view the event from the rear,
The thing that you always will keep on your mind
Is that cow puncher's shirt tail a floppin' behind.

If you've seen some old waddy jest bustin' his neck
To escape from some critter that's got on the peck,
You've discovered two facts, jest between you and I,
That a cow boy can run and a shirt tail can fly.
He knowed what he'd get if he happened to fail,
So he shore didn't stop to arrange his shirt tail.

Them "Levi P. Strauss" is built small in the seat
And a cowpuncher's frame doesn't carry much meat.
He can eat a big breakfast and long before night
He's so empty and hongry that nothin' fits tight.
And besides, he gits rassled and tussled around
Till the best behaved shirt tail won't hardly stay down.

Yes I know it's a fact and beyond any doubt
That a cowpuncher's shirt tail will keep comin' out.
It's the work that they do and the clothes that they wear,
And it's partly perhaps that a cow boy don't care;
So I've had to explain to folks, time and again,
Their shirt tails come out 'cause they caint keep 'em in.

The Creak of the Leather

It's likely that you can remember
A corral at the foot of a hill
Some mornin' along in December
When the air was so cold and so still.
When the frost lay as light as a feather
And the stars had jest blinked out and gone.
Remember the creak of the leather
As you saddled your hoss in the dawn.

When the glow of the sunset had faded
And you reached the corral after night
On a hoss that was weary and jaded
And so hungry yore belt wasn't tight.
You felt about ready to weaken
You knowed you had been a long way
But the old saddle still kep a creakin'
Like it did at the start of the day.

Perhaps you can mind when yore saddle
Was standin' up high at the back
And you started a whale of a battle
When you got the old pony untracked.
How you and the hoss stuck togather
Is a thing you caint hardly explain
And the rattle and creak of the leather
As it met with the jar and the strain.

You have been on a stand in the cedars
When the air was so quiet and dead
Not even some flies and mosquitoes
To buzz and make noise 'round yore head.
You watched for wild hosses or cattle
When the place was as silent as death
But you heard the soft creak of the saddle
Every time the hoss took a breath.

41

And when the round up was workin'
All day you had been ridin' hard
There wasn't a chance of you shirkin'
You was pulled for the second guard
A sad homesick feelin' come sneakin'
As you sung to the cows and the moon
And you heard the old saddle a creakin'
Along to the sound of the tune.

There was times when the sun was shore blazin'
On a perishin' hot summer day
Mirages would keep you a gazin'
And the dust devils danced far away
You cussed at the thirst and the weather
You rode at a slow joggin' trot
And you noticed somehow that the leather
Creaks different when once it gits hot

When yore old and yore eyes have grown hollow
And your hair has a tinge of the snow
But there's always the memories that follow
From the trails of the dim long ago.
There are things that will haunt you forever
You notice that strange as it seems
One sound the soft creak of the leather
Weaves into your memories and dreams.

The Discovery

The morning was clear, but the west wind was chilly;
The high peaks gleamed white, where it recently snowed.
When there passed through this country so rugged and
    hilly,
A grizzled cow-puncher, who scratched as he rode.

The expressions he wore on his face were quite funny—
There were times that he smiled, there were times he
    frowned.
He stopped in a place that was sheltered and sunny—
He reined in his horse, and got down on the ground.

He spread out his "chaps" to protect him from cactus,
And also to keep his clothes out of the dirt;
And then in a way that betrayed former practice,
He started perusing the seams of his shirt.

It made his teeth chatter, but that did not matter—
His skin roughened up in the cold winter breeze;
But he captured some cooties—some diamond black
    beauties—
The kind that he got when he went over-seas.

His present condition was far from delightful
(Although he had been in predicaments worse).
The language he used was both lurid and frightful—
It's awful to hear an old cow-puncher curse!

The habit of wearing these things is contagious,
And to boil woolen clothing is surely a shame;
The things that he threatened to do were outrageous,
In case he found out who was really to blame.

He cursed all the Mexicans, Indians and strangers
(He could not remember of meeting with tramps).
He cursed the cow-waddies and government rangers,
The mess-wagons, bunk-houses, ranches and camps.

That night as he sat by the warm bunk-house fire,
He told all the crew what he found in his shirt.
One hot-headed boy called another a liar,
And grabbed up the poker—his feelings were hurt.

Each "Waddy" put in an emphatic denial,
And cursed all the rest for unpurified bums;
But when it was brought to a search and a trial,
They found the whole outfit polluted with "crums."

They boiled all their clothes, while they grumbled and
    muttered,
And spoke of the things they intended to do;
On their ropes and the fences their bright blankets
    fluttered—
Someone was to blame, but God only knows who.

The Dutch Oven

You mind that old oven so greasy and black,
That we hauled in a wagon or put in a pack.
The biscuits she baked wasn't bad by no means,
And she had the world cheated fer cookin up beans.
If the oven was there you could always git by,
You could bake, you could boil, you could stew, you **could fry**.

When the fire was built she was throwed in to heat
While they peeled the potaters and cut down the meat.
Then the cook put some fire down into a hole.
Next, he set in the oven and put on some coals.
I allus remember the way the cook did
When he took the old "Goncho" and lifted the lid.

He really was graceful at doin' the trick.
The old greasy sackers they just used a stick.
Boy Howdy! We all made a gen'l attack
If the hoss with the dutch oven scattered his pack.
You mind how you lifted your hoss to a lope
And built a long loop in the end of your rope.

You bet them old waddies knowed what to expect.
No biscuits no more if that oven got wrecked.
We didn't know much about prayin' or lovin'
But I reckon we worshipped that greasy old oven.
And the old cowboy smiles when his memory drifts back
To the oven that rode in the wagon or pack.

An Experiment

I'm jest a old hard and fast "Rimmy'
That's allus worked one certain way.
I was talkin' to Eddie and Jimmie,
And it's better to dally they say.
You often have heard people talkin'
That it don't hurt a feller to try.
Now I never was much hand fer knockin',
But I'm willin' to state that's a lie.

It was on the beef hunt last September
I jumped a big three-year-old steer.
He gave me a few to remember,
He went through the bresh like a deer.
He certainly knowed how to do it.
He was leavin' from there like a bat.
But I sez, jest you help yourself to it,
I'll soon be around where you're at.

The hoss I was ridin', I'm sayin,
Was lazy but not very slow.
He had the world cheated fer stayin',
If you'd spur him you bet he could go.
That steer? Hadn't no chance to turn him,
He wasn't the turn around breed.
So I reckoned I'd start in and learn him
By breakin' the critter to lead.

I sent my old loop his direction,
I jerked at it and let my rope cross,
Then I aimed to establish connection
Betwixt that said steer and my hoss.
I dabbed fer my winds on "Old Sally,"
But the hoss sort of shirked and hung back.
I thought I had room fer a dally
But the steer got away with my slack.

Then my whole constitution jest buckles,
Like when somebody tromps on your corn.
Fer the end of my rope and my knuckles,
Was all that I got on the horn.
My hand was all busted and mangled.
Got one crooked finger now. See?
Well, I follered the steer till he tangled,
And got him tied up to a tree.

There is certain sad memories that lingers,
And I reckon that this one will last.
I may break my neck, not my fingers,
But I'll risk it and tie hard and fast.

A Fast Start

They are leavin' from there but they aint goin' far
Or they wouldn't be ridin' as fast as they are.
For even a fuzzy faced kid ort to know
If you want to go far you must start 'em out slow.
Or you'll git every thing your hoss has in his hide
And still be a long ways from the end of your ride.
Jest let him go walkin' along fer a while
A takin' it easy fer over a mile.
Then stop. Git your saddle set right on his back.
And then when you cinch him pull some of the slack.
Gist hitch up your "Levi's" and fix you a smoke.
Like a sensible man and a sho'nough cow poke.
You will soon learn the pace that he travels the best.
Set down in your saddle and he'll do the rest
You will find when you're through, if there's any hoss there
He will last a long time and he'll git you somewhere.

Katherine Field -33

Flankin'

There is work where a feller can do things by halves,
But there's nothin' like that when you start flankin calves.
You want to be sudden. Don't give 'em no hope.
Git that in yore mind when you start down the rope.

Partickler the ones that is husky and large;
You caint tell jest whether they'll jump or they'll charge.
If you miss when he jumps, there's a jerk and a jolt;
Your off of yore feet and he's busted yore holt.

You git kicked in the belly as quick as a flash,
And yore covered with sumpthin' that hits with a splash
You git on yore feet and you see the boys grin,
You grab holt of the rope and go at him ag'in.

He goes high in the air and he kicks and he bawls,
His foot goes inside of yore overalls.
This time you upset him and hold him by chance,
But the critter has tore you half out of yore pants.

You git sore at the crew 'cause they holler and laff,
But you've made fun of hands that got tromped by a calf.
You want to be sudden. Don't give him no hope.
Git that in yore mind when you go down the rope.

49

Ghost Canyon Trail

There are strange tales told of spirits bold,
And the trail to Santa Fe,
There is many a tale of the Chisholm trail,
And the trail to Laramie.
But this is the tale of an obscure trail
That few men travelled on;
Where a spirit was known to ride alone,
'Twixt the midnight hour and dawn.

It would wind and creep through canyons deep
And over the mesa wide.
The men who knew this trail were few,
Where the phantom used to ride.
At times was heard a careless word
Some drinking man let fall,
But 'twas held a joke by the rangeland folk,
That no one believed atall.

I learned the truth from a hardy youth.
He was one of those reckless men
Who could ride in the lead of a night stampede,
Or the dust of the broncho pen.
On a winter night when the stars were bright
And the dying moon was low,
He was holding his course on a jaded horse
And the pace that he made was slow.

The cow horse flinched and cringed, till the **cinch**
Was almost against the ground.
His quivering ears showed deathly fear
And the cow boy looked around.
He felt the thrill of a clammy chill,
As it travelled along his spine,
For he saw at his side a phantom ride,
With never a word or sign.

He kept his place, for he set his pace
To the cow boy's jogging speed.
There came no sound on the frozen ground
From the tread of his phantom steed.
He showed a flash of a long moustache
And a tilted campaign hat.
There straight and strong with stirrups long
The phantom trooper sat.

They were all alone. And the pale moon shone
Through the ghost at the cow boy's side.
His courage fled as he rode with the dead
Alone on the mesa wide.
No sign of flight, no show of fight
The buckaroo displayed,
For slugs of lead won't hurt the dead,
Through the mist of a vapor shade.

With the mesa past they came at last
To a canyon wide and dark,
Where some stone huts stood in the cottonwoods
That had long been an old land mark.
Each ruined shack had a chimney black,
And a roofless crumbling wall.
A living spring was the only thing
That was useful to men atall.

The chilling breeze through the leafless trees,
Gave a dreary dismal moan.
The trooper stayed in the ghastly shade
And the cow boy rode alone.
Strange tales are heard of what occurred
At that place in years gone by,
Ere that restless soul of the night patrol
Rode under the starlit sky.

What the trooper knows, or where he goes,
Nobody has ever found.
But the tale is told of the lone patrol
By the older settlers 'round.
There's a cow boy trim with a face that's grim,
Will never forget that ride
On a winter night in the pale moon light,
By the phantom trooper's side.

The Ghosts at the Diamond Bar

'Twas a winter night at the Diamond Bar,
The wind was blowin' cold.
The Dipper swung 'round the dim North Star
And the night was growin' old.
But I had some wood that was dry and good,
So I let the cold wind whine.
I was safe and snug with a gallon jug
Of Death Valley Slim's moonshine.

Across the stove from where I sat
Stood a figger straight and tall.
He had no coat, he had no hat,
He must have come through the wall.
He pointed away toward a rocky shelf
That was up on the side of a hill.
He was one of the bunch the Injuns skelped
When they raided the old ore mill.

I nodded and passed the gallon jug.
He needed a drink or two.
But he only shrugged and shook his head;
That was sumpthin' he could not do.
I set the jug down on the floor;
Then my eyes popped open wide.
There had been jest one; now a couple more
Was a standin' there by his side.

They would each one point with a ghostly hand
Where my old Harmonica lay.
By signs they made me understand
They wanted that I should play.
So I played 'em "The Grave On The Lone Prairie,"
And "The Dyin' Ranger." too.
And twenty odd ghosts surrounded me
Before I was half way through.

I played 'em the old "Rye Whisky" tune
And they waltzed it 'round and 'round.
But I felt no weight on the floor of the room
And their feet made never a sound.
Then "Rosie O'Grady" and "Over The Waves,"
They waltzed with keen delight.
Them wandering spirits out of their graves
Was havin' a time that night.

They motioned that I should drink once more.
That was easy to understand.
With noiseless feet they stomped the floor
And patted their phantom hands.
When I seen 'em smile I changed my style.
I played old "Larry McGee."
They wanted something with a lilt and swing,
And they stepped it light and free.

But jest as the thing was goin' grand,
There was sumpthin' spoiled the show.
There wasn't a drop in the coal oil can
And the lamp was burnin' low.
I stopped and drunk me a hefty slug
And a thought come to my mind.
I filled the lamp from the moonshine jug
And she blazed like a neon sign.

There was battered hats on the buckaroos.
Old miners with unshaved jaws.
Three Wallapi bucks were in there too,
And a couple Mohave squaws.
The next was the old time "Chicken Reel,"
And you'd orta seen 'em go.
They would jig on the corners before they'd wheel
And give it the heel and toe.

I knew they wouldn't be there fer long.
It would soon be breakin' day.
And I wanted to sing 'em a good old song
Before they went on their way.
So I sung like I had never sung before,
Till the last of the crowd was gone.
And when I opened the ranch house door,
The day was beginning to dawn.

Yes, the desert trails have their own weird tales
That few of us mortals know.
And I'll never forget that crowd I met
On that night so long ago.
Some time I will meet them again, maybe,
Though I don't know where they are.
But why did they come to visit me,
That night at the Diamond Bar?

Katherine Field. 33

High an' Wicked

When they cut you out a bucker why the boys all gathers
    'round
Fer to see the hull performance when you let the hammer
    down,
They will help you while you saddle and they ear him down
    you bet,
Till they git you up a straddle and you tell 'em that yore set.

Then they jump away and holler and they hit him with their
    hat,
And he bucks plum high and wicked weavin' crooked like a
    bat.
When he hits the ground he shakes you, then he lurches through
    the air—
You caint see that broncho no place but you shore can feel he's
    there.

Now you aim to show that critter they's a cow boy on his back,
So you rake him down the shoulders and you pitch the cuss the
    slack.
Then you show the other fellers how you fan 'em with yore lid,
And the old hoss bucks and bellers while you holler like a kid.

Now yore gettin' kinda dizzy and yore feelin' soter shook;
You was sartin you could ride him but you might have been
    mistook.
But his jumps begin to weaken and at last his head appears;
It's a welcome sight old cowboy, is a buckin' hoss's ears.

His Old Clothes

The chuck wagon trailer had just got his card
To attend the spring round up. He stood in the yard
And studied a minute and scratched his gray head,
Then brought in a gunny sack out of the shed.

He emptied it out on the clean kitchen floor
And took a good look at the clothes he once wore.
Yes there was the hat, stained with sweat and with grease
And some faded worn Levis that bagged at the knees.

A brush coat and chaps that were scarred up and wrinkled
And a pair of big spurs that still jingled and tinkled.
A pair of old boots and a heavy wool shirt,
Two long hoggin' strings and a Mexican quirt.

He grinned mighty cheerful and said to his wife,
"I'll give them old waddies the start of their life.
I'll wear my old chaps and my boots and cross L's
I was wunst a brush popper, a rider from Hell."

His wife sure looked wild when she heard what he said.
She begun to git mad, she was sure turnin' red;
Of a sudden she changed and she said with a smile,
"Sure put 'em on Daddy and wear 'em a while.

The first was the shirt. How that old waddy swore.
It jest wouldn't go on and it ripped and it tore.
The boots they jest wouldn't go onto his feet
And the old Levi pants was too small in the seat.

In the last twenty years he had gained forty pound
And the old leather brush coat it wouldn't go 'round.
Now chaps on a street suit don't look very well
And them low oxford shoes isn't built for cross L's.

If he wore decent clothes he could not wear the hat
So his plan to play cow boy was finished at that.
He would have to go dressed like he always had done
Though to wear his old outfit would sure have been fun.

But his woman she really surprised him at that
Fer she got him new boots and a new Stetson hat.
He got in the front seat but she drove the car.
You know how old fellers with younger wives are.

When he got to the round up he met all the boys
And had him a day such as old folks enjoys.
He looked 'em all over and right then he knew
They had all wore the clothes that their wives told them to.

Hook em' Cow

You read of fierce bulls in the stories and books,
But you don't hear a heap 'bout an old cow that hooks.
A bull charges blind, but an old cow is wise.
She keeps her head shakin' and opens her eyes.
If you git to a post I have generally found
She runs right up to it and reaches around.

And yore biddin' fer trouble as shore as yore born
If you git yore old belly mixed up with her horn.
You have seen a cow scatter a whole brandin' crew
When they drug a calf in and the cow follered too.
Think a cow boy caint run? Well you aint seen one sail
When a cow blows her nose on some waddy's shirt tail.

Sometimes when you pull a cow out of a bog
She will charge with a rush like some salty brush hog.
If an old cow gits down 'cause she's weak and she's pore,
If you help git her up she will fight you jest shore.
If you judge by her actions toward hosses and men,
She's by nature a heap like an old settin' hen.

I'll bet you was glad that you wasn't too late
When you lit with yore belly across some old gate,
And an old cow hit right underneath with a crash.
Jest a little more and she'd settled yore hash.
You fell on across, and was mad when you heered
How the rest of them ranahans hollered and cheered.

Yes cows is odd critters; it shore is plum strange.
The pet cows is gentle, but them on the range
Is a sp'ilin' fer fight if they once git a skeer,
Or you make a calf bawl when the old cow can hear.
They're onreasonable cusses I'll tell you right now,
Fer you caint explain much to a fightin' old cow.

60

How a Cow Puncher Rode

I have often been asked by the people I knowed,
To tell 'em the way that a cow puncher rode.
Now them cow hands they didn't all ride jest the same.
They rode a'most every old style you could name.

Of course, most of hands that was workin' around,
Would ride with long stirrups, and straight up and down.
Some rode with 'em medium, some with 'em short.
In fact there was stirrups and len'ths of all sorts.

I know of one feller that quarreled with his brother,
Because he rode one stirrup longer than t'other.
Some stuck their laigs foreward and held their heels low.
Some held their laigs back like, and turned down their toe.

Some held their feet still, but some figity cuss
Would keep kickin' his feet and makin' a fuss.
There was some that set straight, but there's others that humped
Till they set on their hoss in a sort of a lump.

There was some of them riders kep' close to their seat.
While others was half of the time on their feet.
Some bogged on the cantel and rode away back,
While others would jig like they rode on a tack.

There was some kep' their elbows down close to their side.
And others ag'in that would let 'em spread wide.
While some of 'em flopped up their elbows so high,
You would think mebbyso they was tryin' to fly.

There was them that would ride with their hand on the horn.
Some looked plum contented and some looked forlorn.
There was them, fer some reason I couldn't explain,
Whirled a piece of their rope or the end of a rein.

There was some of them fellers set off to one side.
In fact I can't tell how a cow boy did ride.
When I figger it out, there is only one guess.
They rode like they thought they could do it the best.

I'm Hittin' the Trail Tonite

The moon rides high in the cloudless sky
And the stars are shinin' bright
The dark pines show on the hills below
The mountains capped with white.
My spurs they ring and the song I sing
Is set to my horse's stride
We gallop along to an old time song
As out on the trail we ride.

CHORUS.

Oh I'm hittin' the trail tonite tonite
I'm hittin' the trail tonite
My horse is pullin' the bridle reins
And I'm hittin' the trail tonite.
The moon shines down on the rollin' plains
And the tops of the mountains white
My hoss is pullin' the bridle reins
And I'm hittin' the trail tonite.

You can hear the sound as he strikes the ground
On the frozen trail below
His hoof beats hit and he fights the bit
He's slingin' his head to go.
I'll ride the trail till the stars turn pale
And camp at the break of dawn,
Nobody will know which way I go,
They'll only know I'm gone.

I did not try to say good bye
Let somebody else do that,
I'll ride alone and I'll find a home
Wherever I hang my hat.
Let people that set and talk explain
Jest whether I'm wrong or right
My hoss is pullin' the bridle reins
And I'm hittin' the trail tonite.

It Might Have Been Me or
It Might Have Been You

You have heard lots of stories how cow boys behaved,
There was some of them reckless and some of them brave;
And some jest plain waddies that worked with the crew.
Such as might have been me or they might have been you.

But the boys acted different I generally found,
If there chanced to be people hangin' around,
Than they did out alone where nobody could see.
Was it that way with you? It was that way with me.

On the round up a man with a hoss that would buck
Didn't seem to consider he'd met with bad luck.
While the boys helped him saddle he'd laff and he'd joke.
He would pull down his hat and he'd roll up a smoke.

His heart might be poundin' in onder his shirt,
But he'd pull off the blind and he'd give him the quirt.
And he'd ride or git throwed like a real buckaroo.
Yes, that might a been me or it might a been you.

But out in a water lot some where alone
A boy trapped a fresh hoss, a big mean lookin' roan.
How gentle and easy he got in the saddle
Jest to see how he'd act when he once got a straddle.

He eased him around the corral on a walk
And give him a ear full of kind gentle talk
He sure didn't hurry although it was late.
He slid off real careful and opened the gate.

He set about like he was ridin' on eggs.
And he felt him out light with the calves of his legs.
Yes he jest stole a ride fer the fust mile or two.
Well, that might a been me and it might a been you.

Judgement Day

Once I dremt while I was sleepin'
That the earth had passed away,
And the boss of all creation
Made a work on Judgment Day.
They was folks of every color
They was folks of every breed
And they cut 'em into bunches
'Cordin' to their race and creed.

Top hand angels done the cuttin'
They knowed how to handle things,
Some would change and help the others
While they'd smoke and rest their wings.
And I seed a bunch of fellers
They was holdin' on the side.
Grazin' soter loose and easy
And the angels workin' wide.

He had judged and classed the others
By a book of rules he used,
Then he called out to the angels
"Now bring on the buckaroos!"
Angels bunched and shoved 'em foreward,
Some surprised but not dismayed.
Amblin' up to face the judgment
Came that grizzled wild brigade.

Each one pulled his hat on tighter.
That they done from habit's force,
It's a trick of most rough riders
When they mount a buckin' horse.
Some was young and some was older,
Some walked with a limpin' stride.
Some still had the high heeled boots on
They was wearin' when they died.

They all stood in line to answer
Fer the way they'd spent their days.
And they faced the boss of Heaven
With a cool and level gaze.
And the boss of all creation
Give them boys a kerful look,
And sez to a top hand angel,
"Bring me out that range law book."

Well, I turned and asked an angel
Why the judgment book was changed,
And they judged that bunch of cow boys
By the laws that ruled the range.
And he answered very solemn
That the reason was because
You could never judge a cow boy
By another feller's laws.

That Letter

I rode to that box a settin' on a post beside the trail,
That our outfit used fur gettin' all their messages and mail.
There I got a little letter and the envelope was pink,
It shore set me feelin' better but it soter made me think.
Yes the feelin' was surprisin' onderneath my Stetson hat.
I could feel my hair a risin' like the bristles of a cat.

Well I tore the letter open and I read it through and
    through.
All the time I was a hopin' I would savvy what to do.
Men is quick upon the trigger, come tangle ups and fights,
But a woman, you caint figger what she means by what she
    writes.
It was purty and invitin' like a sunny day in spring,
She had done a heap of writin' but she hadn't said a thing.

Now, when men folks start to writin' you can mostly
    onderstand,
And the stuff that thay're a sightin' stands out plain jestlike
    a brand
They don't never do no playin' they've a sort of sudden way,
For they start right in by sayin' what they started out to say.
Men is given to expressin' what they mean, right then and
    there,
But a woman keeps you guessin' till your mind goes
    everywhere.

Fer a spell I'd do some thinkin' then I'd start agin and read;
I kept frownin' and a blinkin' till at last I got her lead.
In that letter there was lurkin' jest one simple plain idee.
When I got my mind a workin' it was plain enough to see.
Fer she said her and her mother, come a Saturday next week
Would be over with her brother to the dance on Turkey
    Creek.

On the start, you see, I never had no notion what she meant.
She had fixed it up right clever in the way the letter went.
Man! I shore did whoop and beller when the idee hit me fair,
She would come without no feller and she aimed to meet
     me there.
It shore made me like her better fer that bashful gal of mine,
Went and built that whole durned letter, jest to write that
     single line.

The Line Camp

You rode into the line camp 'bout the time the sun went down;
Got the load from off yore pack hoss, throwed yore saddle
     on the ground.
You was glad the man before you had a heart and chopped
     some wood,
But when you went inside the shack things wasn't quite so
     good.

You found dead flies and cobwebs and lots of things like that.
One stove laig broke, some wore out clothes, and plenty sign
     of rats.
You got a rock and propped the stove and soter cleaned the
     junk.
Then drug yore tarp and blankets in and throwed them on the
     bunk.

Next thing you brought your grub inside and built a fire on.
There wasn't any lantern and the candles all was gone.
Well, you tore up some flannin rags and made a right good
    wick,
And scouted out a lard pail lid—you waddies know the trick.

You melted taller or some lard, it didn't matter which;
And you was all primed up to go, you had a "Kitchen Bitch."
The coffee cooked, the meat got fried, and you was cheerful
    hearted.

Because you had been there before and soter liked the shack.
The same old nails to hang yore clothes, the rafters smoky
    black.
And when you got yore supper et you lit yore pipe agin,
Then propped yore feet up by the stove and let the heat soak
    in.

Before you slept you went to see your night hoss in the trap.
You crawled into yore blankets and you didn't give a rap.
The night wind blowed real soft and slow and you was all
    alone;
It was nothin' but a line camp but to you 'twas home sweet
    home.

That Little Blue Roan

Most all of you boys have rode hosses like that.
He wasn't too thin but he never got fat.
The old breed that had a moustache on the lip;
He was high at the wethers and low at the hip.
His ears always up, he had wicked bright eyes
And don't you furgit he was plenty cow wise.

His ears and his fets and his pasterns was black
And a stripe of the same run the length of his back.
Cold mornin's he'd buck, and he allus would kick
No hoss fer a kid or a man that was sick.
But Lord what a bundle of muscle and bone;
A hoss fer a cow boy, that little blue roan.

For afternoon work or for handlin' a herd,
He could turn any thing but a lizzard or bird.
For ropin' outside how that cuss could move out.
He was to 'em before they knowed what 'twas about.
And runnin' down hill didn't faize him aytall.
He was like a buck goat and he never did fall.

One day in the foot hills he give me a break
He saved me from makin' a awful mistake,
I was ridin' along at a slow easy pace,
Takin' stock of the critters that used in that place,
When I spied a big heifer without any brand.
How the boys ever missed her I don't onderstand.
Fer none of the stock in that country was wild,
It was like takin' candy away from a child.

She never knowed jest what I had on my mind
Till I bedded her down on the end of my twine.
I had wropped her toes up in an old hoggin' string,
And was buildin' a fire to heat up my ring.
I figgered you see I was there all alone
Till I happened to notice that little blue roan.

That hoss he was usin' his eyes and his ears
And I figgered right now there was somebody near.
He seemed to be watchin' a bunch of pinon,
And I shore took a hint from that little blue roan.

Instead of my brand, well, I run on another.
I used the same brand that was on the calf's mother.
I branded her right pulled her up by the tail
With a kick in the rump for to make the brute sail.
I had branded her proper and marked both her ears,
When out of the pinons two cow men appears.

They both turned the critter and got a good look
While I wrote the brand down in my old tally book.
There was nothin to do so they rode up and spoke
And we all three set down fer a sociable smoke.
The one owned the critter I'd happened to brand,
He thanked me of course and we grinned and shook hands
Which he mightn't have done if he only had known
The warnin' I got from that little blue roan.

The Long-Eared Bull

The long eared bull was three years old.
He was swift and cunning, strong and bold;
His horns were wide and his neck was full,
He walked with pride, did long eared bull.
He bellowed the notes of his challenge call
Till they echoed back from the mountain wall.

One day there chanced to hear him sing,
A waddy who dangled a wicked string,
When he caught a glimpse of the singer's ears
His lips went shut like a pair of shears.
They were both untouched and stood out wide.
He knew that no brand adorned that hide.

He made quite sure that his cinch was tight,
For he knew he was starting a full grown fight.
He built a loop for a hasty swing
And spurred his horse toward the mountain king.
Away they went like a pair of deer,
The buckaroo and the big long ear.

He cut down the distance yard by yard,
Till the bull found out he was crowded hard.
He thought he'd retreated far enough
So he whirled about with a charge and snuff.
The cow horse dodged with a sidewise leap.
The cow boy threw and he caught him deep.

He caught the bull with a "Shot pouch hold"
On the ground the horse and rider rolled.
The puncher saw that it was no use
So he dropped his dallies and turned him loose.
The bull was off like a prairie gale
With a dragging rope and a waving tail.

The cow boy hung his head in shame;
He had lost his rope and his horse was lame;
His hands were skinned and his clothes were torn,
He had gone for wool and had come back shorn.
For if either of them got the wool,
The honors lay with the long eared bull.

Now a fat old cow man came one day
On a gentle old flea bitten gray.
This wise old gentleman had a hunch
He could humor him in, if he took the bunch.
So he worked them along at an easy pace
And avoided all signs of a fight or race.

He kept well back and circled wide
To corral the bull and to brand his hide.
But just as they got where the brush was thick,
The long eared bull threw a trump on the trick.
When they got in the open the bull was gone
And the rest of the bunch were travelling on.

A beardless youngster, lithe and slim,
Was riding one day by the canyon's rim.
The happiest youngster in the land,
For just one week he owned a brand.
He saw the bull and how he smiled,
For the soul of a cow man was in that child.

He descended the hill with a cheerful heart,
For little he knew the fight he'd start.
His horse had been ridden some before
But was hardly wise to the hackamore.
Yet he felt his pulses throb with hope
As he tied the end of his old grass rope.

Well over his saddle horn he humped
And took to the race when the long ear jumped.
He was one of the kind that never lean back,
He grabbed his horse and he pitched him the slack,
He rapped his flanks with the ringing steel
While the long eared bull shook a nasty heel.

He built a loop that was big and wide,
He made a throw but the broncho shied.
Then he set right back and buried his tail
And that button thought he had hooked a whale.
Down went the horse—the youngster fell
And he used some words that don't print well.

His face was white but his blood was up,
And he stayed with the fight like a bull dog pup.
As they buck and bellow, plunge and pull;
The broncho horse and the long eared bull.
For the rope was tied and the saddle big
Was cinched with the old time "Rimmy" rig.

The kid gave a squeal of joy and thanks
As the rope went under the long ear's flanks.
The horse went bucking off to the right,
To the left the long ear took his flight.
When they took up the slack the two of them flopped
Right down on their backs and the old rope popped.

The kid was there with an agile spring
His teeth still clinched on his "Hoggin' string"
He won by a hair but he did not fail,
For he got his hold on the long ear's tail.
He tied him down and he swelled with pride
As he run his brand on the glossy hide.

The boy has lived to be old and gray.
He has been successful in every way.
It wasn't by luck, it wasn't by pull,
But the spirit that branded the long eared bull.
In spite of the fall that ended the ride
And the whirlwind fight on the mountain side.

The Long Horn Speaks

The old long horn looked at the prize winning steer,
And he grumbled, "What sort of thing is this here?
He ain't got no laigs and his body is big,
I sort of suspicion he's crossed with pig.
Now me, I can run, I can gore, I can kick,
But that feller's too clumsy fer all of them tricks.

They are breedin' such crittres and callin' 'em steers!
Why the horns that he's got ain't as long as my ears.
I caint figger what he'd have done in my day.
They wouldn't have stuffed him with grain and hay;
Nor have polished his horns and have fixed up his hoofs,
And slept him on beddin' in onder the roofs.

Who'd have curried his hide and have fuzzed up his tail?
Not none of them riders that drove the long trail.
They'd have found mighty quick jest how far he could jump
When they jerked a few doubles of rope off his rump.
And to me, it occurs, he would not look so slick
With his tail full of burrs and his hide full of ticks.

I wonder jest what that fat feller would think,
If he lived on short grass and walked miles for a drink.
And wintered outdoors in the sleet and the snow.
He wouldn't look much like he does at the show.
I wouldn't be like him; no, not if I could.
I caint figger out why they think he's so good.

His little short laigs and his white baby face—
I could finish him off in a fight or a race.
They've his whole fam'ly history in writin', and still,
He ain't fit for nothin' exceptin' to kill.
And all of them judges that thinks they're so wise,
They look at that critter and give him first prize.

The Lost Flannins

Old greasy John Blair had a shootin' affair
'Way back in the year ninety three.
I don't know if it's true, but I'll tell it to you,
Just the same as John told it to me.

Said Greasy, as he tipped back his chair,
"That story shore puts me in mind
Of a suit of red flannins I got down to Shannon's,
And some trouble I had with O'Brien.

You see I rode line with this Jimmy O'Brien,
That winter I shore do recall
We got, as you knows, our tobacker and clothes,
When we went out of town in the fall.

We was both plenty tough, but the weather was rough,
And it made us go prowl our war sacks.
All the clothes we could find, either his'n or mine,
We put 'em right onto our backs.

Them red flannins of mine was most sartinly fine,
I didn't begrudge what they cost.
But a turrible thing happened 'long toward spring,
My suit of red flannins got lost.

There was jest I and Jim so I blamed it on him,
And Jim, right away he got tough.
He was never right mild, and when once he riled,
I am present to state he talked rough.

Well a'most every day we'd get started some way,
About where them red flannins had gone.
And the more that I thought, the plum shorer I got,
That my old pardner Jim had 'em on.

We had et a big bait and was startin' out late;
The weather was perishin' cold.
I walked up to him and sez, look a here Jim,
I want them red flannins you stoled.

Jim's eyes they got mean,and he sez, we'll come clean.
I been hearin' this talk quite a spell.
And I caint onderstand how a reasonable man,
Would be wantin' red flannins in Hell.

It wasn't no fun, fer he took to his gun,
And we shot till the cabin was fogged.
The chinckin' shore flew where the bullets cut through,
While some others plowed into the logs.

When the smoke cleared away, there my old pardner lay,
And I sez to him, Mister O'Brien,
Since at last you have got to aplace where it's hot,
I'll be takin' them flannins of mine.

I onbuttoned his clothes and what do you suppose?
He didn't have any onderwear.
I searched all around and they couldn't be found.
Them red flannins wasn't no where.

'Bout the time the grass rose I began sheddin' clothes.
My onderwear started to stick.
It clogged up my sweat when I got overhet,
So I took me a swim in the crick.

When I dove in at fust I washed off some loose dust,
And then quite a coating of muck.
I finally come to a layer of tough gum,
But I still was as dry as a duck.

Well I swum around some till I soaked through the gum,
And the water got into my pores.
It shore made me shivver, chilled plum to the liver,
I waded out onto the shore.

I stood in the sun; I'm a son of a gun;
I thought in my soul I'd a died.
I had them clothes on that I figgered was gone,
They'd been plastered down next to my hide.

I know Jim O'Brien that old pardner of mine;
He's a settin' down there on the coals.
And I reckon he'll wait right close up to the gate
And be ready to bull dog my soul.

It drives me to drink every time that I think
Of Jim fixin' it up with Old Satan.
I know all these years he's been backin' his ears,
And jest itchin' and watchin' and waitin'.

I might make a try for a home in the sky,
But that wouldn't be treatin' Jim fair.
I made the mistake so I'll give him a break,
And we'll settle the matter down there.

The Marking Knife

He sheds his big hat when he gits into town
And his boots ain't so good when he's walkin' around,
But there's part of his outfit he don't throw away.
He's had it fer years and it's with him to stay.
For down in his pocket the rest of his life
The cow puncher carries his old markin' knife.

He could use that sharp blade and beyond all belief.
With nothin' but that he could butcher a beef.
If a sliver got into his hand or his thumb
He would use that old knife blade and out the thing come.
It did his repair work at night in the camps,
He used fer markin' and whitlin' out clamps.

One time his hoss slipped on a muddy side hill
And he thought that he'd never git clear from that spill.
The hoss lit on his leg and he mighty well knew
By the feel of the stirrup, his foot had gone through.
He held the hoss down by the head with the reins;
He battled and fought, but kept using his brains.

He got to the pocket he had in his chaps,
Got his knife, and then cut off his leitigo straps.
When the hoss had got up and he'd saved his own life,
He fixed up the wreck with his old markin' knife.
In plenty of ways any cow puncher found
'Twas a might good thing to have handy around.

With his knife he could allus find sumpthin' to do,
'Twas his tool kit, newspaper and radio, too.
He used whenever he worked or he played,
He was allus at home if he had that old blade.
He handles that knife and he dreams of the past,
And he keeps his old markin' knife plum to the last.

The Midwinter Bath

I'm home plenty early, I reckon—
It's too soon to start cookin' grub,
So before I begin with my bakin'
I'll take me a bath in that tub.

I'll build up a plenty big fire,
And git all the kittles well filled;
If there's one thing that I don't admire,
It's gittin' in water that's chilled.

That wind is some cold and plum nosey—
It's comin' right in through the cracks—
But I'll fix the place up warm and cozy,
And stuff that broke window with sacks.

Wow! Wow! But it sure makes you shiver—
A man wouldn't really suppose
It would chill him plum into the liver,
The minute he takes off his clothes.

Now, there is old Billy McRady—
He's eighty, and got his third wife.
She's quite a respectable lady—
And old Bill never bathed in his life.

When did I bathe last—I remember,
Although I ain't put the date down—
I had one the first of November,
The last time I went into town.

It's weak'nin', a man can't deny it,
But I'm takin' a chance, anyway;
It won't hurt a feller to try it,
For this here is Volunteen day.

I'll git that new bar of Fels Napthy
And doll myself sweet an' clean,
And come out all purty an' happy—
Like somebody's sweet Volunteen.

Ouch! Say, but my feet must be tender—
But then a man should understand,
When he feels of the water, remember,
That his feet ain't as tough as his hand.
I don't think it hurts your endurance,
Except when a feller jest soaks,
For baths is a common occurrence
Among the society folks.

The men, kids and the women
Put on little short-legged skirts,
And goes in the ocean a swimmin';
They don't reckon as how that it hurts.

I've read about them in "The Tattler."
Great goodness! jest look at them heels;
I'm sheddin' my hide like a rattler—
It's turrible how a man peels.

I'v got some clean under-clothes ready,
But the others is still warm for me;
I'll go at this thing sort of steady—
Too much of it mightn't agree.

Les' see, now—November, December—
And this here is Volunteen Day;
I'll mark down the date and remember
I'm good 'till the first of next May.

It may cause a feller to weaken,
It may sort of shorten Life's path;
But I'll tell you right here, plainly speakin',
I sure do enjoy a good bath!

Moccaison Mick

Old Moccaison Mick of Scorpion creek
Was wild in the early day.
The part he played in each Injun raid
Would carry yore breath away.
With howls and yelps he had lifted skelps.
He had danced to the tom tom drums.
But he ceased to fight when his hair got white,
And the teeth fell out of his gums.

But he still felt young and he chawed his tongue
When the women folks come around.
And late in life he married a wife
That weighed three hundred pound.
There was rolls of fat where the lady sat.
She had a substantial figger.
Her front begins with a row of chins,
And each chin gits bigger and bigger.

One day Mick laid asleep in the shade,
And he heard his woman shout.
"I am snake bit Mick Oh Lord come quick
And suck the pizen out!"
Mick dropped his jaw when he looked and saw
Where the rattle snake had bit.
He blushed with shame and wasn't game.
He throwed down his hand and quit.

His face was red and scratched his head
In onder his greasy hat.
"I have done some turrible things," he said,
"But I never done nothin' like that."
She yelled "I'm sick—come on be quick!
Do hurry and save my life!"
But old Mick said as he shook his head,
"No, I'll git me another wife."

Katherine Field. JV

New Boots

I got my new boots and they fit me jest right.
Of course all the other hands sez they're too tight.
Some sez they're too small, and some sez that they figger
They're shore big enough, but my feet's a heap bigger.

Last night a dumb waddy was springin' a joke,
How I pulled the tape measure so tight that it broke.
I've got the Lumbago—the hands all got cute.
Said I ruint my back pullin' on my new boots.

The boss sez the heels is too high fer his likin'.
Well he shore ort to know I don't use boots fer hikin'.
They fit me jest perfect. The tops is stitched fine
The bosses boots never was e'kul to mine.

I ordered them boots and I paid the cash down
And they's no better boots in the country around.
I know why them fellers won't let me alone.
When they look at my boots they're ashamed of their own.

The Old Night Hawk

I am up tonight in the pinnacles bold
Where the rim towers high.
Where the air is clear and the wind blows cold,
And there's only the horses and I.
The valley swims like a silver sea
In the light of the big full moon,
And strong and clear there comes to me
The lilt of the first guard's tune.

The fire at camp is burning bright,
Cook's got more wood than he needs.
They'll be telling some windy tales tonight
Of races and big stampedes.
I'm gettin' too old fer that line of talk.
The desperaders they've knowed,
Their wonderful methods of handling stock,
And the fellers they've seen get throwed.

I guess I'm a dog that's had his day,
Though I still am quick and strong.
My hair and my beard have both turned gray,
And I reckon I've lived too long.
None of 'em know me but that old cook, Ed,
And never a word he'll say.
My story will stick in his old gray head
Till the break of the Judgment Day.

What's that I see a walkin' fast?
It's a hoss a slippin' through.
He was tryin' to make it out through the pass;
Come mighty near doin' it too.
Git back there! What are you tryin' to do?
You hadn't a chance to bolt.
Old boy I was wranglin' a bunch like you
Before you was even a colt.

It's later now. The guard has changed.
One voice is clear and strong.
He's singin' a tune of the old time range—
I always did like that song.
It takes me back to when I was young
And the memories came through my head,
Of the times I have heard that old song sung
By voices now long since dead.

I have travelled better than half my trail.
I am well down the further slope.
I have seen my dreams and ambitions fail,
And memory replaces hope.
It must be true, fer I've heard it said,
That only the good die young.
The tough old cusses like me and Ed
Must stay till the last dog's hung.

I used to shrink when I thought of the past
And some of the things I have known.
I took to drink, but now at last,
I'd far rather be alone.
It's strange how quick that a night goes by,
Fir I live in the days of old.
Up here where there's only the hosses and I;
Up in the pinnacles bold.

The two short years that I ceased to roam,
And I led a contented life.
Then trouble came and I left my home,
And I never have heard of my wife.
The years that I spent in a prison cell
When I went by another name;
For life is a mixture of Heaven and Hell
To a feller that plays the game.

They'd better lay off of that wrangler kid
They've give him about enough.
He looks like a pardner of mine once did.
He's the kind that a man can't bluff.
They'll find that they are making a big mistake
If they once git him overhet;
And they'll give him as good as an even break,
Or I'm takin' a hand, you bet.

Look, there in the East is the Mornin' Star.
It shines with a firy glow,
Till it looks like the end of a big cigar,
But it hasn't got far to go.
Just like the people that make a flash.
They don't stand much of a run.
Come bustin in with a sweep and dash
When most of the work is done.

I can see the East is gettin' gray.
I'll gather the hosses soon;
And faint from the valley far away
Comes the drone of the last guard's tune.
Yes, life is just like the night-herd's song,
As the long years come and go.
You start with a swing that is free and strong,
And finish up tired and slow.

I reckon the hosses all are here.
I can see that T-bar blue,
And the buckskin hoss with the one split ear;
I've got 'em all. Ninety two.
Just listen to how they roll the rocks—
These sure are rough old trails.
But then, if they can't slide down on their hocks,
They can coast along on their tails.

The Wrangler Kid is out with his rope,
He seldom misses a throw.
Will he make a cow hand? Well I hope,
If they give him half a show.
They are throwin' the rope corral around,
The hosses crowd in like sheep.
I reckon I'll swaller my breakfast down
And try to furgit and sleep.

Yes, I've lived my life and I've took a chance,
Regardless of law or vow.
I've played the game and I've had my dance,
And I'm payin' the fiddler now.

The Old Time Christmas

I liked the way we used to do, when cattle was plenty and folks
    was few.
The people gathered frum far and near, and they barbacued
    a big fat steer.
The kids tried stayin' awake because, they reckoned they might
    ketch Santa Claus.
Next mornin' you'd wake 'em up to see, what he'd been and
    put on the Christmas tree.

It was Christmas then fer the rich and pore, and every ranch
    was an open door.
The waddy that came on a company hoss was treated the same
    as the owner and boss.
Nobody seemed to have a care, you was in among friends or
    you wasn't there.

Some had new boots, which they'd shore admire when they
warmed their feet in front of the fire.

And the wimmin folks had new clothes too, but not like the
wimmin of these days do.

Some times a drifter came riding in, some feller that never was
seen agin.

And each Christmas day as the years went on we used to
wonder where they'd gone.

I like to recall the Christmas night. The tops of the mountains
capped with white.

The stars so bright they seemed to blaze, and the foothills swum
in a silver haze.

Them good old days is past and gone. The time and the world
and the change goes on,

And you cain't do things like you used to do when cattle was
plenty and folks was few.

An Old Western Town

An old western town lay asleep in the sun
Of a long summer day that was then almost done.
The shadows were long and the hosses stood 'round
Sort of restin' one leg and their head hangin' down.
Two cow punchers down at the "Last Chance" saloon
Was tryin' to sing. They was both out of tune.
At one end of the street that was dusty and narrow
A scratchin the dirt was some chickens and sparrows.

The dogs slept in the shade and the people they strolled
Like they felt plum contented in body and soul.
If you looked just a little ways off to the west
You could see the high mountains with snow on their crest.
The shadows of clouds drifted over the flat
And it shore made a right purty pitcher at that.
A drunken cow puncher was ready to go
And he figgered he'd ort to put on a big show.
He spurred and he hollered and shot his six gun,
And he aimed to take out with his hoss on the run;
But he didn't remember his cinches was slack
Until after he got his old pony ontracked.
That cow hoss he started to buck and to bawl
And got rid of that cow puncher saddle and all.
And before that drunk waddy got clear of the wreck
He was bit by two dogs, which he didn't expect.

The hoss he bucked into a long hitchin' rack
Where a team was hitched to a wagon raired back.
They lit out a draggin' the old rattle trap
And swingin' the broke ends of two hitchin' straps.
A whole lot of people come from everywhere
The sparrows and chickens they took to the air.
The kids made for cover, the women all screamed
And the dogs was all chasin, that runaway team.

A feller run out like some man allus did
A yellin' and jumpin' and wavin' his lid.
When the hosses got close why the man lost his nerve.
He got out of the way but he made the team swerve.
They tore down the porch posts in front of the store.
They busted the winder and several things more.
They was off of their feet when at last they got stopped
Piled up in a heap with the wagon on top.

They was fast in the harness, one hoss nearly strangled,
But the crowd went to work and they got 'em untangled,
But just when they started to take 'em away
The storekeeper come out with plenty to say.
His place had been wrecked, but what made it worse still
The man with the team owed the store man a bill.
He swore he would take it all out of his hide
He shore wasn't bluffin, he got in and tried.

But most of the citizens present they reckoned
That the storekeeper come off a mighty pore second.
The town marshall come with his badge and his gun
Just in time for a drink when the whole thing was done.
The sun soon went down. Then a few golden streaks
From the afterglow showed on the snowy peaks.
The kerosene lamps shed a soft yellow light
Where the town folks was cookin' their supper that night.

'Twas a real western night with no fog or no haze
The stars hung in clusters so bright that they blazed.
Some neighbors they gathered to visit and talk
You could hear the slow foot steps along the board walk.
There sprung up a soft gentle breeze from the west
One after another the lights went to rest
And the curtain of night settled quietly down
On that best of all places, an old western town.

Our Boss

He started young and he drifted far—
The owner out at the Diamond-Bar.
He has cattle grazing on many a hill,
But down in his heart he's a cow-boy still.

Though other owners put on airs,
It's little for style that our boss cares;
He wears his boots and his leather chaps,
And everybody calls him "Tap."

He bandies jokes and exchanges news,
As he rides the range with his buckaroos;
He sits his horse with a careless grace,
And rides at a stockman's jogging pace.

But the horses he rides all come of a breed
That are bred for mettle and built for speed.
The thing that he really most enjoys
Is a horse round-up with a bunch of boys.

It's then he rides at a pace that kills,
Through the open flats and the rugged hills;
With spurs set close and with flying reins—
Like he rode when a boy on the Texas plains.

Or else, when he jumps big mountain steers,
That have dodged the round-up for several years—
Down comes his rope, and away they dash,
While the hoof-beats ring and the cedars crash,
Till the bellowing steer on the mountain side,
Proclaims the fact that he's roped and tied.

I have seen him riding at racing speed—
Singing in front of a mad stampede—
As calmly as most old gentlemen do,
When sitting at church in a rented pew.

If he did retire and settle down
He would waste away in the sheltered town
Where he couldn't hear the cattle bawl,
The horses neigh, and the coyote's call.
He was raised on the range, and there he stayed—
One of the boys of the old brigade.

Out of Turn

Have you been in a bunk house or 'round a chuck wagon,
Where all of the fellers was talkin' and braggin'?
'Bout the bronks they had busted and men they'd seen throwed,
And the hosses that bucked and the fellers that rode.
And before you got through runnin' off at the head
You had said a few things that you ortn't to said.
Fer they cut you a couple of hosses right soon,
That would hang their tail over the top of the moon.

Do you ever remember when you was a kid,
You got terribly stuck on a gal? Yes you did.
One day you found sumpthin' that shore made you glad.
A big unbranded calf that belonged to her dad.
You allowed you would do the old man a good turn,
And you'd visit a spell with that father of hern.
You built a big loop and you charged with a rush.
The whole bunch of cattle went into the brush.

And when you got some of them out in the clear,
You found yourself right up behind a long ear.
You branded him up, but 'twas no time to laff.
He run to his mother—You'd got the wrong calf.

Kid like you said nothin' about the mistake,
And that wasn't givin' the old man a break.
So the feller you'd picked fer a fatherinlaw
Got cussed fer a cow thief and punched in the jaw.

Have you bragged a whole lot on some feller you knowed,
'Bout the way that he roped and the way that he rode?
You crowed a whole lot about what he could do
And afriend of yours hired him 'fore you got through.

He got bucked off his hosses, got lost on the range;
Stole other boy's socks when he needed a change.
He camped at a line camp and burnt down the shack,
He borrowed some money he never paid back;
And when you tried takin' it out on his hide
He give you a whale of a lickin' beside.

Remember the times that yore hosses would stray
And you'd saddle a hoss and hunt fer 'em all day?
And when you got home again, tired and late,
You found 'em a grazin' 'round close to the gate.

Remember the time when you got a new hat?
Then you took a few drinks and felt real prowd at that.
Goin' home in the dark, well, the hat blowed away
And you aint never heard of it plum to this day.

When you sometimes set smokin' and thinkin' at night,
You remember a few things that happend all right.
Old friends and old faces whose memory will last.
Old jokes and old troubles creep out of the past.
There were streaks of hard luck that were really a blessin',
Fer some times a mistake was a valuable lesson,
Of course at the time you was shore plenty mad,
But you think of it now, and it wasn't so bad.

Rain

It's sumpthin' a feller caint hardly explain
The way that a cow puncher feels about rain.
It makes the feed grow and it fills up the tanks,
And genreally speakin' he'd orta give thanks.
He wakes up some night when the rain hits his bed
And pulls the tarpolian up over his head.
It's warm when it rains and he gits overhet
And he lays there all night in a miserable sweat.

He wakes up next mornin', his boots is all soaked
Jest laugh that one off if you think it's a joke.
He pulls at the lugs and he stomps and he knocks
Till he drives both his feet through the toes of his socks.
He gits his boots on but you know how it feels;
No toes in his socks and them wrinkled up heels.
When he goes to ketch out it ain't no easy trick
With a rope that is wet and as stiff as a stick.

He dabs for his hoss and he makes a good snare
But the hoss downs his head and backs right out from there.
Fer a cow pony knows you caint tighten a loop
When you ketch with a rope that's as stiff as a hoop.
When he gits saddled up he must climb up and ride
And that wets the last dry spot he had on his hide.
The hoss starts to buck but that cow boy is set
Fer a man's hard to throw when his saddle is wet.

All day he keeps ridin' the flats and the hills,
A slippin' and slidin' and likely he spills.
When he gits into camp he must stand up to eat,
And his clothes is all wet from his head to his feet.
He stands 'round the fire, he cusses and smokes,
Fer he hates to git into a bed that's all soaked.
But his slicker's wet through fer it's old any way,
And there's mighty few slickers turns water all day.

And while he turns in, and as strange as it seems
He goes off to sleep and he sweats and he steams.
Next mornin' it's clear and the wind's blowin' sharp
He shivers and crawls out from under his tarp.
By the time he eats breakfast he's feelin' all right
And his bed will dry out by a couple more nights.
But the old saddle blankets are still cold and wet,
And the hoss humps his back and looks wicked you bet.

Old cow boy is tired, he's stiff and he's sore,
He's had lots of trouble, he don't want no more.
So he takes that old pony and leads him around
Till he gits his back warm and the saddle sets down.
Fer the man that's been rained on two nights and a day,
Ain't lookin' fer trouble; he ain't built that way.
He wants feed and water but let me explain,
A waddy ain't comf'tble out in the rain.

Katherine Field - 54.

Ridin' Fence

Ridin' along at a easy walk with your steeples and hammer
   and pliers.
Keepin' a watch fer the tracks of stock or the weeds blowed
   up on the wires.
You find some sign of coyotes, too, and plenty of rabbit
   tracks.
And down in the wash some calves crawled thru and
   scraped the hair off their backs.

You must fix the gate on the other side along where the
    road goes through.
The past'rs big. It's a good long ride and they's allus a
    heap to do.
You find a place where a big old bull went through in that
    patch of oak.
They's a picket out and some steeples pulled and a couple
    of wires broke.

Some folks had camped at the Hillside spring, been there
    for a couple of days.
The boss don't like that sort of thing. They might kill a
    beef, he says.
Before you finish it gits plum dark. You caint see to do
    things right.
So you pile up some rocks to make a mark and ride on
    home in the night.

Fence ridin' jobs aint allus snaps. I never did call it fun.
The worst thing about it is perhaps that yore never exactly
    done.
But any feller that's got good sense can figger the whole
    affair.
If nothin' went wrong with a string of fence, he wouldn't
    be needed there.

Second Guard

You are sleepin' in your hot roll when some body kicks your
    tarp.
When you roll out of your blankets why the wind feels cold
    and sharp.
It was Tex come in to wake you, but he needn't kick so hard.
Ain't no need to kill a feller 'cause he's pulled fer second
    guard.
Johnnie's over at the fire with the old black coffee pot.
Coffee like all hands admire, plenty stout and plenty hot.
You both drink a shot of coffee and you roll and light a
    smoke.
Then you crawl up on your night hoss. Neither one of you
    has spoke.

You relieve old Lonesome Barry, him that's got the squeaky
    voice.
Allus singin' Annie Larry, Lord he makes a rotten noise.
Well, you sing "The Texas Ranger" and you give your hoss
    the rein.
Johnny starts around to meet you singin' "Good Bye Lizy
    Jane."

Your old hoss walks slow and steady, with his nose close to
the ground.
Though your ears is cocked and ready, still you don't git nary
sound,
'Cept the creakin' of your saddle and the singin'   of your
pard,
And the breathin' of the cattle, as you ride the second guard.

Stars is out so bright they're blazin' and sometimes you see one
fall.
Joshuas a standin' 'round you like old men that's bent and tall.
You can see the old moon risin' and you hear the sand rats play.
Second guard is awful lonesome, but it's int'restin' some way.

Now you wish there was a country where they allus had good
feed.
Where there ain't no buckin' hosses and the cattle don't
stampede.
Pretty women and good likker, and where shootin cranks,
ain't barred.
Where the cooks all make good biscuits, and there ain't no
second guard.

The Silk Shirt

You recollect that pink silk shirt you bought so long ago,
The time us boys went into town to see the rodeo.
The second day you had it, it begun to show the dirt.
When you wore it after sun down you would git so cold
    you hurt.

But the first time that we branded, well, it didn't look so
    new.
It appeared plum second handed; tore and smeared with
    blood and goo.
Next day, well, you jumped some hosses and you had to
    make a ride,
When you took 'em off the mesa and come down the
    mountain side.

When they took you through the cedars, why yore shirt
    begun to tear.
By the time you hit the slide rock jest a part of it was
    there.
But the thing was tore to ribbons, and yore hide was
    scratched, oh gosh!
When you once got through the cat claw that was growin'
    in the wash.

At the old home ranch that evenin' you was settin' on a
    rail.
You still had the cuffs and collar and a portion of the tail,
So you put yore old brush jumper on. 'Twas full of sweat
    and dirt,
But 'twas built to hold a cow boy better than a pink silk
    shirt.

Springtime

They're roundin' the hosses up agin and startin' the work
    fer spring.
They're gittin' the old remuda in and cuttin' the hands
    their string.
A couple of boys is out from town and one of 'em talks a lot.
You wait till he lets the hammer down on a few of the
    mounts he's got.

All winter long they've been runnin' out, they know every
    rock and trail.
They are bad as the broncs, or jest about, and wild as a
    bunch of quail.
When you jump a bunch it's shore a race, they're makin'
    you play yore stack.
You ride till the wind shore whips yore face and hammers
    yore hat brim back.

But it won't be long till they're all smoothed down, that is
    as a gen'l thing
The bad uns will go to Sandy Brown, he's ridin' the snaky
    string.
Fer me, he's welcome to all that kind, I figger jest like the boss.
There's nothin' that suits me half so fine as ridin' a well
    broke hoss.

Stan

Saint Peter stood at the Golden Gate
Givin' the crowd the works.
The people was there from ev'ry state,
Missourians, Jews and Turks.
They were all in line and things went fine
Till the system got upset.
Up rode a man by the name of Stan
From the Brewery Gulch Gazette.

"Git this through yore head," Saint Peter said,
So fur yore the only one
That has dast come here in his ridin' gear   ....
On a onnery wall eyed dunn.
You said yore a dude, but yore rough and rude,
And I'd have you onderstand,
You have got the walk, the way and the talk,
Of a regular old rough hand.

You ain't allowed in the Gospel crowd.
One reason you caint get through,
We've got some folks don't like yore jokes,
From the W.C.T.U.
Yore a goin' to clear right out from here,
Both you and that wall eyed brute.
I'm a shippin' you South to the parminint drouth.
Git into that left hand chute!"

Stan raked the dunn and the son of a gun
Raired straight as a dyin' whale.
When he hit the ground his head come down
And he shore did swaller his tail.
Stan waved his hat and fanned his fat
And give 'em the cow boy yell.
And you ort to have heered how the Devil cheered
As he stood on the gates of Hell.

'Twas a clever trick and he worked it slick.
They found it out too late.
He steered the wreck with a spur in his neck,
Right in through the open gate.
Saints shuffled their feet on the golden street
When they ran behind telephone poles.
Stan was first to ride plum high and wide
Through the city of ransomed souls.

There could nothin' out run that wall eyed dunn;
They went through the town right quick.
He last was seen in the pasters green
A headin' right up the crick.
Old Soloman Wise of the sportin' guys,
Went over and cashed a bet.
He had bet on the man by the name of Stan,
From the Brewery Gulch Gazette.

Thinkin'

It's an easy job herdin' "Parada." Yore old hoss is standin'
    close bye.
You are watchin' the drift of the shadders that's made by
    the clowds in the sky.
There's a breeze blowin' over the mesa. It pulls at the brim
    of yore hat.
You feel soter careless and lazy, but it sets you to thinkin'
    at that.

Of the towns where the folks herd together with sidewalks
and plenty of light.
They are sheltered and out of the weather, they sleep in a
house every night.
There's plenty of good drinkin' water and places to eat
night and day.
They live like a man really oughter, you wish you was livin'
that way.

You know lots of outfits and bosses but that's jest a cow
puncher's chance.
You begin when you're young wranglin' hosses, and wind
up a cook at some ranch.
You figger it's really a pity. You've been on the range since
a kid.
You would shore like to go to the City, but what could you
do if you did?

Your idees git twisted and broken. You reach fer your
papers and sack.
You reckon you'll do some more smokin', you turn with
the wind to your back.
How things will work out there's no knowin' but the cattle
are startin' to stray,
So you'd better git up and be goin' fer thinkin' don't help
anyway.

The Time to Decide

Did you ever stand on the ledges,
On the brink of the great plateau,
And look from their jagged edges
On the country that lay below?

When your vision met no resistance
And nothing to stop your gaze,
Till the mountain peaks in the distance
Stood wrapped in a purple haze.

On the winding water courses
And the trails on the mountain sides,
Where you guided your patient horses
On your long and lonesome rides.

When you saw Earth's open pages,
And you seemed to understand
As you gazed on the work of ages,
Rugged and rough, but grand.

There, the things that you thought were strongest
And the things that you thought were great,
And for which you had striven longest,
Seemed to carry but little weight.

While the things that were always nearer,
The things that you thought were small;
Seemed to stand out grander and clearer.
As you looked from the mountain wall.

While you're gazing on such a vision
And your outlook is clear and wide,
If you have to make a decision,
That's the time and place to decide.

Although you return to the city
And mingle again with the throng;
Though your heart may be softened by pity,
Or biter from strife and wrong.

Though others should laugh in dirision,
And the voice of the past grow dim;
Yet, stick to the cool decision
That you made on the mountain's rim.

The Tinker

There is one sort of cow hand that never is idle.
He is weavin' a cinch or he's fixin' a bridle;
He sits by the wagon or in the corral
And makes him a breast rig or braids a bosalle.

He has a grass rope and a rieta too,
With a quirt and hackamore nearly bran new.
He's got him a headstall that's made with a blind
And novelty spur rowells of different kinds.

He has got neckin' halters and spare hoggin' strings,
He has taps fer his stirrups and tossels and things.
A few extra jaw straps fer onder his bit;
A dehornin' saw and a shoein' outfit.

If he's in at the home ranch or out in the camps
He is workin' on hobbles and twitches and clamps.
Awls, needles, and waxends, and gauges, it's facts
The stuff he has gathered fills three gunny sacks.

He has new patent things to change stirrups perhaps.
And new patent fasteners fer latigo straps.
You boys have all seen him. He's one of the breed.
That has got every thing a cow puncher don't need.

He never works hard but he has lots of friends.
He is willing to give, he is willing to lend.
He supplies the whole oufit, and the bosses have found
It's mighty convenient to have him around.

Turnin' 'em

It looks like this feller had been on a stand,
He was out runnin' hosses with some other hand.
He's been savin' his hoss and a holdin' right still,
Till they went to break past at the foot of the hill.

The other boy's job, was to jump 'em and send 'em.
This old boy was waitin' there, ready to bend 'em.
From the looks of the way he is comin' in sight,
I reckon they had the thing timed about right.

A cow puncher knows that the pony he rides,
Must carry a man and a saddle besides.
It would be a big job to run wild hosses down
When they've got a long start and don't carry a pound.

But, "there's tricks to all trades." So the old sayin' goes,
And, there's quite a few tricks that a hoss runner knows.
Range hosses are foxy and know what to do,
But good team work will take 'em before they get through.

The Veiled Rider

It was down at the home ranch, a bunch of cow pokes
Got on an old hoss that was only half broke.
They saddled him up and they hazed him around,
But none of them rode him. They stayed on the ground.

The cook he laffed at 'em and laffed mighty hard.
Then the boys they allowed that the cook wasn't barred.
But it shore did amaze 'em to see the cook crawl
Right up in the saddle, yes apron and all.

The hoss took to buckin' all over the place.
The cook's apron flew up and covered his face.
His stirrups was long and he had to pull leather,
But the cook was on top when they finished together.

One waddy he grins and remarked to the boss,
"Seems they blindfold the rider now, 'stead of the hoss."
The cook looked at the boss sorter mournful and said,
"This whole crew aint wuth seven dollars a head.

I buried my face in my apron all right,
But I done it to shut out the pitiful sight.
Like a bunch of fresh toad frogs that been rained down.
Them pore rannies hoppin' and yappin' around.

I will own up right now, I'm a cranky old cook,
But there's sights where really upsets me to look.
That had been out and cooked for a bunch of real hands.
And an outfit like that would disgust any man."

Wet Boots

A cowboy goes onder a turrible strain,
When he tries to wear boots that's been soaked in the rain.
He pulls and he wiggles, and after he's tried,
He gits him some flour and sprinkles inside .

Then he gits him two jack knives; puts one in each lug,
And he stomps and he pulls till his eyes starts to bug.
Next he tries a broom handle—a awful mistake.
Which same he finds out when he feels the lug break.

The toes and the heels they bust out of his socks,
And it's awful to hear how that cowpuncher talks.
He opens his knife and it shore is a sin,
Fer he cuts his new boots till his feet will go in.

I reckon old timer, you know how he feels.
You have kicked bunk house walls and the chuck wagon
    wheels.
And you know when yore older, there's nothin' to gain
From buyin' tight boots if you work in the rain.

When Conners Rode Rep
For The Lord

One time they was givin' a big work fer souls,
They was plum over stocked so they say.
The owners all over that section was told
To come and help take 'em away.

The Devil he come and brought with him three hands
That was nearly as smart as their boss.
They was there representin' the old Pitch Fork brand
Buck Connors was there fer The Cross.

All three of them hands and the Devil was wise,
They thought they was runnin' things, but,
Buck Connors he pulled his hat down to his eyes
And rode in and started the cut.

All four of them fellers sez never a word,
They figgered they might git a break.
They watch everything that come out of the herd,
But Buck never made a mistake.

When he finished his cut he rode up to the boss
And he sez, "Well I reckon I'm through.
I got everything that belong to the Cross
And I'm turnin' it over to you."

So the throw back went home to the ranch in the sky
And the Devil he never once scored.
Not even Old Satan hisself could git by
When Buck Connors rode rep fer the Lord.

When They've Finished Shipping Cattle in the Fall

Though you're not exactly blue,
Yet you don't feel like you do
In the winter, or the long hot summer days.
For your feelin's and the weather,
Seem to sort of go together,
And you're quiet in the dreamy autumn haze.
When the last big steer is goaded
Down the chute, and safely loaded;
And the summer crew has ceased to hit the ball;
When a feller starts a draggin'
To the home ranch with the wagon—
When they've finished shippin' cattle in the fall.

Only two men left a standin'
On the job for winter brandin',
And your pardner he's a loafin' at your side.
With a bran new saddle creakin',
Neither one of you is speakin',
And you feel it's goin to be a silent ride.
But you savvy one another,
For you know him like a brother.
He is friendly but he's quiet, that is all;
He is thinkin' while he's draggin'
To the home ranch with the wagon—
When they've finished shippin' cattle in the fall.

And the saddle hosses stringin'
At an easy walk a swingin'
In behind the old chuck wagon movin' slow.
They are weary gaunt and jaded
With the mud and brush they've waded,
And they settled down to business long ago.
Not a hoss is feelin' sporty,

Not a hoss is actin' snorty;
In the spring the brutes was full of buck and bawl;
But they're gentle, when they're draggin'
To the home ranch with the wagon—
When they've finished shippin' cattle in the fall.

And the cook leads the retreat
Up there on his wagon seat,
With his hat pulled way down forrud on his head.
Used to make that old team hustle,
Now he hardly moves a muscle,
And a feller might imagine he was dead,
'Cept his old cob pope is smokin'
As he lets his team go pokin'
Hittin' all the humps and hollers in the road.
No the cook has not been drinkin'
He's just settin' there and thinkin'
'Bout the places and the people that he knowed
You can see the dust a trailin'
And two little clouds a sailin',
And a big mirage like lakes and timber tall.
To the home ranch with the wagon—
When they've finished shippin' cattle in the fall.

When you make the camp that night,
Though the fire is burnin' bright,
Yet nobody seems to have a lot to say.
In the spring you sung and hollered,
Now you git your supper swallered
And you crawl into your blankets right away.

Then you watch the stars a shinin'
Up there in the soft blue linin'
And you sniff the frosty night air clear and cool.
You can hear the night hoss shiftin'
And your memory starts a driftin'
To the little village where you went to school.

With its narrow gravel streets
And the kids you used to meet,
And the common where you used to play baseball.
Now you're far away and draggin'
To the home ranch with the wagon—
For they've finished shippin' cattle in the fall.

And your school boy sweetheart too,
With her eyes of honest blue—
Best performer in the old home talent show.
You was nothin' but a kid
But you liked, sure you did—
Lord! And that was over thirty years ago.
Then your memory starts to roam
From Old Mexico to Nome.
From the Rio Grande to the Powder River,
Of the things you seen and done,
Some of them was lots of fun
And a lot of other things they make you shiver.
'Bout that boy by name of Reid
That was killed in a stampede,
'Twas away up north you helped to dig his grave,
And your old friend Jim the boss
That got tangled with a hoss,
And the fellers couldn't reach in time to save.

You was there when Ed got hisn,
Boy that killed him's still in prison,
And old Lucky George is rich and livin' high.
Poor old Tom, he come off worst,
Got his leg broke, died of thirst
Lord but that must be an awful way to die.

Then them winters at the ranches,
And the old time country dances,
Everybody there was sociable and gay.

Used to lead 'em down the middle
Jest a prancin' to the fiddle
Never thought of going home till the break of day

No there ain't no chance for sleepin'
For the memories come a creepin'
And sometimes you think you hear the voices call;
When a feller starts a draggin'
To the home ranch with the wagon—
When they've finished shippin' cattle in the fall.

When You're Throwed

If a feller's been a straddle since He's big enough to ride,
And has had to throw a saddle onto every sort of hide;
Though it's nothin' they take pride in, most of fellers I have
    knowed,
If they ever done much ridin,' has at various times got
throwed.

It perhaps is when you're startin' on a round up some fine day,
That you feel a bit onsartin 'bout some little wall eyed bay.
Fer he swells to beat the nation while yore cinchin' up the
    slack,
And he keeps a elevation in your saddle at the back.
He starts rairin' and a jumpin' and he strikes when you git
    near.
But you cuss him and you thump him till you git him by the
ear.
Then your right hand grabs the saddle and you ketch a stirrup
    too,
And you aim to light astraddle like a wholly buckaroo.

But he drops his head and switches and he gives a back'ards
jump.
Out of reach your stirrup twitches and your right spur grabs
his rump.
And, "Stay with him!" shouts some feller. But you know it's
hope forlorn.
And you feel a streak of yeller as you choke the saddle horn.

Then you feel one rein a droppin' and you know he's got his
head,
And your shirt tail's out and floppin' and the saddle pulls like
lead.
Then it ain't no use a tryin' for your spurs begin to slip
Now you're upside down and flyin' and the horn tears from
your grip.

Then you feel a vague sensation as upon the ground you roll,
Like a vi'lent separation' twixt your body and your soul.
And you land agin a hummick where you lay and gap fer
breath,
And there's sumpthin' grips your stummick like the awful
clutch of death.

Yes the landscape round you totters when at last you try to
stand,
And you're shaky on your trotters and your mouth is full of
sand.
They all swear you beat a circus or a hoochy koochy dance,
Moppin' up the canon's surface with the busom of your pants.

There's fellers gives perscriptions how them bronchos should
be rode.
But there's few that gives descriptions of the times when they
got throwed.

Who Told the Biggest

One night a bunch of buckaroos
Were gathered 'round a fire;
And each one wished to air his views
Before he should retire.

They talked about the world's advance,
They argued on reforms,
Until somebody just by chance
Began to talk of storms.

"One time," remarked old Angus Greame,
"The year I worked for Law,
In Utah, why a cloudburst came—
The worst I ever saw.

It washed the soil all off the knobs
The boulders jumped and bounded,
And seven fellers lost their jobs
On 'count of bein' drownded.

It rained so hard, Lord bless your souls,
That when it let up, why,
The water from the gopher holes
Rebounded six foot high."

A lank Missourian gave a shrug
And slowly shook his head.
He bit a chew off his plug
As if he chewed on bread.

"I 'low," he said, and then he spat
A dozen feet or so,
"It rained some down where I was at
A couple years ago.

It rained a hour mighty hard
It drowned our Jersey bull;
The wagon stood out in the yard,
It rained the box most full.

It lacked of comin' to the top,
A inch, or thereabout;
I reckon 'twould have filled it up,
But I'd left the end gate out."

"I'll tell you what, the fact remains,"
We heard a deep voice say.
Our blizzards sure beats all your rains
Back home in Ioway.

One time a blizzard hit our town
Along in nineteen two.
The stuff that wasn't fastened down
Jest riz right up and flew.

The roof came off the city hall
And tumbled 'round and 'round.
It blowed our mule again the wall
Ten feet above the ground.

It blowed so hard that I'll declare
You couldn't git your breath;
It held that pore old mule up there
Until he starved to death."

One boy rubbed Old Johnny Bais's head,
A smile was on his face.
"That's what the jackass got," he said,
"Fer stayin' in one place."

"That's right," replied old Johnny Bais,
"It often happens so.
I stay whare I was born and raised;
I ain't no jackass though."

A boy from Arizona spoke,
"I'll tell you something strange;
It's sure the truth, and not no joke,
It happened on this range.

I had a yellow dog called Snap;
One day I tied him up.
He opened up his mouth to gap,
A whirlwind hit that pup.

It picked him up and spun him 'round
And rolled him all about.
It left him layin' on the ground
Jest turned plum inside out."

A man from Kansas then spoke up.
"I don't exactly know
About a whirlwind and a pup,
I know how cyclones go,

My Pa and Ma took up a claim
Along in Ninety-three.
With sister Sue and sister Mame,
And brother Bill and me.

We built a house and barn and well,
The place did look immense.
We broke up sod fer quite a spell
And built some wire fence.

And then one day a cyclone hit—
I heard our old cow beller;
The house went up and never lit
And left us in the cellar.

The barn got up and danced a jig,
The wire fence broke loose.
Our little poll and chiny pig
Flew circles like a goose.

Down came a hoss and then a boot
Close follered by a houn'.
It blowed our well plum out by root
And turned it upside down.

My mother fainted from the scare,
So did my sister Sue.
We hadn't water there;
We couldn't bring 'em to.

Us boys we started on the run
And with us went the houn'
But when we got there we was done,
The well was upside down.

I had a bucket, Bill a cup,
I don't know where we got 'em
We found the well was wrong side up—
The water in the bottom.

We couldn't reach it if we tried,
Dad got to lookin' sadder.
My brother Bill sot down and cried;
I run to git a ladder.

And jest as I was gittin' back
The lightnin' hit the well
Right on the bottom side ker whack,
And blowed it all to—well,

That's jest about the worst cyclone
I ever chanced to see.
We used to talk of it at home;
My brother Bill and me."
"That may be so," said Old Man Carns,
"Of ourse I won't deny,
Some of you fellers jest told yarns,
But someone told a lie."

The Willow Creek Wedding

So you think it's sort of funny
Bill got such a handsome wife?
I know how it happened sonny,
And it was, you bet your life.
Twenty years ago tomorrow
On a Wednesday of the week,
We stirred up some joy and sorrow
Over there on Willow creek.

It was Old Joe Norton's daughter
Started things to move and buzz,
Fer no woman hadn't oughter
Be as purty as she wuz.
And my pal, our broncho twister,
Called him Colorado Jim,
Seemed to like that little sister,
And she seemed right fond of him.

But her folks soon stopped their buzzin'.
They objected on the score
That he'd killed her father's cousin,
Half a dozen years before.
Well that finished up their courtin'
But folks gossiped like they will,
Fer that little Jessie Norton
Started goin' round with Bill.

Jim he didn't seem down hearted
Though us boys did kid him some;
And I noticed that he started
Gittin' letters—how they come.
When a bunch of letters landed
Every other one we saw,
Would be mighty plainly branded
With the name of "James McGraw."

Now the school marm was a widder
And she stayed at Norton's house.
She was never any kidder,
She was quiet as a mouse.
But our boss, first time he met her
Sure declared upon the spot
That he aimed to try and get her,
And he hoped she could be got.

He'd a buggy and two hosses,
Always kept 'em fat and sleek,
And that outfit of the boss's
Often went to Willow creek.
It created quite a ripple
When into our camp one night
Come old Jim Buchanan Whipple,
Givin' out the big invite.

There would be a surenough weddin',
Barbacue fer all the mob,
And old travlin' Parson Teddin'
Would be there to do the job.
Everybody was invited
To the weddin' and the dance;
Fer to see them two united
And to shake our feet and prance.

Norton's house it was too little,
And too fur back in the hills,
So they sent word by old Whipple
That they'd pull it off at Bill's.
On the weddin' day we started,
Jim was nowhere to be seen;
So we thought he was down hearted
And was feelin' sort of mean.

We got there in plenty season
And we turned our hosses out,
And we saw no special reason
Why we shouldn't look about.
Our onneddicated vision
Saw a sight that made us thrill
But we come to the decision
That the thing we saw was Bill.

'Twas his sisters that had dressed him,
And his new white shirt was b'iled;
Wore a suit so tight it pressed him,
And his hair was smooth and 'iled.
Like a colt that's finished sheddin'—
Oh he surely did look sleek
When they fixed him fer his weddin'
Over there on Willow Creek.

Then our boss drove in a flyin'
With the school marm and the bride,
And there wasn't no denyin'
He was all blowed up with pride.
They'd the school marm in the middle,
And they said they aimed to go
Fer to git an extra fiddle
At the house of Andy Roe.

Well we waited and we waited,
Till it wasn't any joke.
Young Tom Graham hesitated,
Then he rose right up and spoke.
"I don't like to mention trouble,"
Tommy sez, "But you folks knows
They've had time enough and double
To git back from Andy Roe's.

I'll jest git my hoss and foller
Fer as strange as it may seem,
I am game to bet a dollar
They've had trouble with that team."
We all looked in Bill's direction,
Then somebody sez to him;
"Everybody in this section
Is accounted fer but Jim."

Then a big bay hoss come swingin'
Up the canon into view,
With the Parson on him singin'
Like a drunken buckaroo.
Talked jest like some old cow waddy,
You could tell he'd had some booze;
Shakin' hands with everybody
And a tellin' all the news.

"Folks!" declared old Parson Teddin
"Listen to me if you can,
I was headed fer this weddin'
When I met a hold up man.
But it turned out fine and dandy
Like a lot of other jokes,
Fur he took me up to Andy's
And I married four young folks.

One as purty little critter
As a feller ever spied.
Oh I never will forgit her;
And Haw! Haw! I kissed the bride.
We'd some toddy at the weddin'
Oh it was the best of jokes."
Then old Bill gasps: "Parson Teddin
What's the name of them there folks?"

"Well," the parson answered gaily,
"Them two gals I never saw;
But one feller's name was Bailey,
And the other's was McGraw."
Bill displayed some agitation
When he heard what had been done.
He made hostile demonstrations
And he went and got his gun.

Bill, I sez, put up that weepin.
Don't you make that sort of play
Less you calculate on sleepin'
Till the resurection day.
You was never much fer fightin'
Them's the words I sez to him.
And you're tanglin' with the lightnin'
When you git your gun fer Jim.

Then up spoke old Johnny Brady,
"Bill you jest keep on your hat
Jessie ain't the sort of lady
That would pull a trick like that.
Some folks may have got united,
Things sounds queer I must confess,
But I wouldn't git excited
Till I had a talk with Jess."

But the boys begun to holler
And the gals begun to smile;
Bill got hot around the collar
And got madder all the while.
There was sure an awful racket
Fer the boys begun to rear,
Till a gal named Sally Brackett
Stepped right out and took the floor.

There was once when she got tangled
And old Bill had rescued her.
She was bein' drug, and dangled
From a cord cinch by a spur.
So she always sort of reckoned
That she owed old Bill a debt;
She was stirred up in a second
And she spoke right out you bet.

Sally hadn't any mother,
Grew up in the hills, that's all.
Used to work beside her brother
Wearin' boots and overalls.
Jest eighteen and full of grit,
And we knew one thing was sartin.
Sally Brackett wouldn't quit.

She was white and awful rattled—
First real dress she ever wore,
But she set her jaw for battle
And to even up the score.
Anybody that was human
Couldn't help but let her speak.
She had growed into a woman,
That wild gal frum Bowlder Creek.

"Folks!" she says, "I ain't a knockin'
On the ways of any one
But what I consider shockin'
Is the way that Bill's been done.
Yes, you boys can stand there grinnin'
Like a bunch of silly apes;
None of you could make a winnin'
So it's only sour grapes.

Everyone of you that's livin',
Would have swapped his chance for heaven
Fer a chance to marry Jess.
Though she made her own selection,
Like a woman mostly will,
Any gal in this here section
Should be prowd to marry Bill.

He's dealt square with everybody
And with all his neighbors here,
Now you poor bow legged cow waddies
Want to stand around and sneer.
Yes, you started in to twit him,
You're on Jim's and Jessie's side;
But you bet I'll never quite him,
If he likes, I'll be the bride.

Bill he stepped right out beside her
And he took her by the hand,
And I heard one rough old rider
Swear that Brackett gal was grand.
So the parson done the hitchin'
And the boys cheered fit to kill;
Sally sure looked plum bewitchin'
When she led the first quadrille.

When I'd look at Jessie's mother,
She appeared to be right sad.
But I noticed that her brother
Was plum wide awake and bad.
Jessie's dad was like a mourner,
Never joinin' in the jokes.
I set with him in a corner—
I was fond of Jessie's folks.

There had been a heavy shower,
And the sun was out again.
When, as purty as a flower,
Little Jess come walkin' in.
Well the things that they was sayin'
Seemed to stop right then and there,
And the fiddles stopped a playin'
And we all begun to stare.

"Folks," she says, "I'm awful sorry
To be gettin' here so late.
But I couldn't make 'em hurry
And I didn't want to wait.
I'd no idee what was brewin'
When I left a while ago,
But there's sure been sumpthin' doin'
Over there at Andy Roe's.

Jim McGraw held up the parson,
It was fun you bet your life.
Bailey's married to Miss Larsen,
And Jim's got the cutest wife.
Fer you see I run accrost her
When I made that trip back East
Jim's first sweet heart, he had lost her
And you know she's Andy's neice.

They was hitched up when I started,
They'll be in here soon I hope.
I took Jim's hoss and departed;
Come the whole way in a lope.
'Twasn't right to keep you waitin'
And I don't go much on jokes—"
Then she started hesitatin'
And sez, "What's the matter folks?"

Then I looked at Jessie's mother,
Saw her face was hard and white,
And her Father and her Brother
Was jest sp'ilin' fer a fight.
'Bout that time the Old Man Brackett
And I knowed there'd be a racket
If they got him on the peck.

So I sez to Jessie's mother,
Take that little gal away.
You two savvys one another;
Tell her what's took place today.
And in case she wants to beller
Why she's ort to be alone,
'Stead of 'mongst a bunch of fellers
In another woman's home.

Well, we set around in silence,
'Cause you know how people are.
I was glad there'd been no vi'lence
In the whole affair so far.
Jess came back and she'd been cryin'
But her voice was clear and slow.
"Folks," she sez, "I ain't denyin'
Things looked bad a while ago.
Everybody in this valley
Was mistaken 'Bout that trick,
So it left a chance fer Sally—
Sally Brackett's sort of quick.

Since they're playin' ladies' choices,
And they seem to be in luck,
If there's no dissentin' voices,
Why, I'd like to marry Buck.
That's of course if Buck is willing—"

And her face got awful red;
I could feel my back a chillin'
And the joy went to my head.

I was prowder than a turkey,
And I answered with a yell
If she wanted me fer jerky
I'd be suited mighty well.
Parson! I sez, come and tie us
'Fore I lose this streak of luck.
But a voice sez right close by us
She won't never quit you Buck."

"I could see how things was layin',
Bill's so jealous he's the bunk.
So I kept them folks a stayin'
And I got the parson drunk.
Bill he's sort of slow a startin'
Seems to kinda hesitate.
But the school marm she was sartin
Sally Brackett wouldn't wait."

There beside me stood the waddy,
He was wiry tall and slim,
That had give the parson toddy.
It was Colorado Jim.
That's the story to a letter,
And I'm here to state it's true.
All alive and doin' better
Than we ever hoped to do.

Yes, Bill's wife she's sure a wonder,
And that school marm she was wise.
But son, don't you make no blunder,
It was me that drawed first prize.

Women Drivers

The motor car made women drivers, they say,
But they had women drivers in yours and my day.
Mind when you and yore Ma stayed to hold the ranch down,
And you took the spring wagon and went into town.

You couldn't start out till the hosses was found.
They was not really lost, they just wasn't around.
You wrangled the canyon and got quite a few,
And she picked out a team that she reckoned would do.

The one was half gentle, the other wild.
He'd been worked a few times but they said he'd been sp'ild.
Well you loaded yore hobbles, yore fry pan and things,
In a tarp you tied down with some old hoggin' strings.

You turned the team out in the paster that night,
And got up the next mornin' as soon as 'twas light.
Got the gentle hoss harnessed and ready to go,
Then yore Ma she was ready to put on the show.

She roped out the wild one and snubbed him up clost.
You helped her to harness him tied to a post.
You recollect yet how you nearly got kicked
When you pulled the old belly band through with a stick.

You hitched him up blindfolded, tied in the gate
Fer she knowed when he started he mightent go straight.
Then yore Ma she allowed it was safer to put
A rope through the hame ring and down to his foot.

Then she sez to you, you was eleven years old,
"Son don't pull that foot rope ntil you are told."
She got in the wagon to start on the trip,
With her foot on the brake, with the lines and the whip.

Then you climbed up beside her and done the last thing.
You jerked that there blindfold away with a string.
I'll say that he lunged, and he kicked and he jumped,
But he way that she welted his flanks and his rump.

Boy! You went down the canyon a bouncin' and flyin'
And you knowed you was headed fer town or fer Zion.
Fer the first half a mile 'twas a whale of a fight
She was just five feet two, but she drove him all right.

It wasn't so long till he got steadied down,
And you and yore mother was goin' to town.
Yes, she wore a long dress and a bonnet and shawl,
But they had women drivers them days, after all.